Adventures of

No Place Like Nome

Book 5

Published by Alaska Adventure Books

Anchor Point, Alaska 99556

www.AlaskaAdventureBooks.com

By Matt Snader

Notes From Readers

Many thanks to everyone who has sent me notes and feedback on the books! I thought I would share a sampling of them, I have way too many to include them all, but we do enjoy reading every one, well most of them, anyway:

"An 18 wheeler would be a bigger billboard for advertising" -Reader in Maryland (I'm personally leaning towards a school bus or motorhome-Matt)

"Don't buy cheap unsafe airplanes! We still want more books…" Reader in Columbus, Ohio

"Anything the next book is about will surely be interesting! Keep up the good work!" Abraham and Fern, from Iowa

"I have a suggestion on finding gold! Search out spots that have small water-falls or eddys, gold is heavy and tends to collect at these areas first." Franklin, from Virginia

"Don't care what story comes next, just keep them coming." Reader from Missouri

"I admire your patient wife. I don't blame her for putting her foot down and drawing the line sometimes!" Joseph from Kentucky

"Say Matt, if you grew some hair on your head and wore a runner hat, it would look a lot more Alasky." David from Michigan

I received a lot of positive feedback on the many pictures, but one or two people complained I had too many pictures...so I guess you can't please everyone. However the people liking the pictures outnumbered the people not liking the pictures 30:1, so we'll keep putting in lots of pictures!

Feel free to send any feedback, comments or suggestions to:
Matt Snader
PO Box 988
Anchor Point, AK 99556

Or email sales@AlaskaAdventureBooks.com. If you email you are much more likely to get a response, as then I don't have to buy stamps. You can also fax us at 717-255-0300.

Photography credits: I lost track of who took what picture, but if you see an exceptional photo just figure it was taken by Missie Sauder, of Missie D. D. Photography.

MISSIE D. Photography

2

Table of Contents

Notes on Marlene's Cookbook

I think Marlene did an excellent job with her cookbook. We were not sure if we were going to add Marlene's cookbook *The Snader Family Alaskan Cookbook* as part of the book series, but my book mentors encouraged me to. I am glad we did, as Marlene's story, which is in the cookbook, is as much a part of the series as mine is. I helped do the layout, and assisted her in writing it, but it is her words, with perhaps a touch of my influence. I couldn't help but wonder at the part titled "How Do I Cope With Alaska." It almost made it sound like she wasn't head over heels in love with Alaska.

She also balked at my photography suggestions, insisting that guns not be used as props. Equally distained were some of my recipe suggestions, especially the ones for dog biscuits. And, it was only with a lot of convincing that she let me put in the Bannock recipe. Marlene claimed none of her other recipes books had pictures of burnt food. She quickly shot down the idea of posing the Alaskan Malamutes with any of the food. In hindsight, that was probably a good idea. They will quickly eat any food close by, and are difficult to restrain. She may have been right. Hairy, drooling dogs don't make good food props.

I am pleased with Marlene's cookbook. I think it turned out well. And it is geared towards women, so I think her décor choices for the photography may have been for the best. However, we made a terrible mistake. On page 82 we put the WRONG recipe in for BBQ Corn Chip Salad! Our sincerest apologies. We have included the correct recipe. This would explain why your BBQ Corn Chip Salad did not look like our picture in the cook book!

Stuffed Pepper Soup can be seen on page 107 of Marlene's cookbook (without the gun or bullets). One day Marlene was busy and told me to take pictures, so this is what I came up with

BBQ Corn Chip Salad

Ingredients

Salad

6 cup lettuce

1 1/2 cup Honey BBQ twists

1/4 cup onion diced

1/2 cup bacon crumbled

3/4 cup cheese

Dressing

1/4 cup sugar

1/2 cup oil

1 T mayonnaise

1 1/2 T vinegar

1 T water

1/2 tsp salt

1/4 tsp onion powder

2 tsp mustard

pepper to taste

Mix dressing ingredients together, add to salad immediately before serving.

Foreword
By Josh Snader

When Matt asked me to write the foreword for his new book, I agreed. I seem to get sucked into many of Matt's money making schemes (I'm his younger brother so naturally this is the case). He comes up with the big ideas and lets me grind my fingers to the bone doing the work while he collects the money. It's a good setup for him, and I'm not complaining about Matt - I'm complaining about my own intelligence. In actuality, Matt has gone through a lot to get to where he is. Then again, if you read the last four or five or twenty books (I'm losing track how many he has written) you know all about the ordeals he and his family have gone through so they could live in a shack in the middle of nowhere. I suspect Matt just wanted me to take up a couple pages of text so he didn't have to write as much himself but that's OK. I actually enjoy the opportunity to get back at my brother.

The problem with writing is that you actually need something to write about. You can't sit down at a keyboard and go, "hmmm…" and then come up with a humorous story about eating breakfast cereal every morning. People don't like reading it, and I can't stay awake long enough to write it. I had put the foreword ideas on a back burner in my mind to simmer. The back burner in my mind is a cluttered place since many pots and pans are competing for space. I usually just wait until life requires me to turn up the heat on an issue and then I yank that particular pot to the front burner and turn the knob up to 11. It's not a good way to cook and it hasn't been working in life either. At any rate – good or bad – the foreword idea was stacked on top of some others in the back of my mind.

Then, before I even got done completing one of Matt's projects, he sucked me into another one. He called me up one day although I didn't know it was him calling me. He has switched phone numbers so often I quit bothering to update his contact in my phone. I answer the phone.

"Hello?"

"Oh hi Josh, this is Matt."

"Oh great!" I put my head in my hands and start sobbing uncontrollably.

"It's nice to hear such emotion at the sound of my name." Matt is impressed with the deep level of our relationship.

"Oh boy, oh boy." I know it's a frantic idea when Matt calls me. Typically he just emails me with his ideas and I just put them on the back burner without hesitation. When he calls, however, it's so important to him that he can't wait for an email response. This means I can't let it simmer until it evaporates away. I have to act on it.

"What can I do for you?" I ask.

"How does a trip to Alaska sound?" Matt offers me a baited hook. Every man has his price. Mine happens to be the current value of the airfare between my current location and Alaska.

As it turns out, Matt had convinced one of his friends to buy a huge swath of land near his cabin. The plan was to build rental cabins on it and then rent them out at discounted rates to tourists who had more brains than money (a common trait of Alaska tourists). This also tripled the land that was available for Matt to hunt on so I suspect he probably had ulterior motives when he sold his friend on the cabin idea.

Many things transpired on the trip to Alaska. One of which included building a cabin complete with working doors and windows, much to the surprise of everyone involved. I feel what happened when we tried to go fishing, though, is an accurate snapshot of much of Matt's life.

Matt was insistent on fishing. More so than building cabins, obviously, our purpose in Alaska was to eat halibut. This requires a boat since swimming with halibut tackle is difficult. Now, Matt has only 3 boats which was a problem, Matt claimed.

"You need at least 4 boats," he explained. "That way you always have one that works. I only have 3 so it may take a little work but we'll get one working. Shouldn't be a problem."

I raised an eyebrow, thinking of all the previous times I had heard the same optimism from Matt about his boats. It was usually unfounded optimism. There is about a one in a hundred chances of a boat working. Since we only had 3 boats the odds were not in our favor.

Matt pointed at his 27 foot boat, perched high on a rickety old boat trailer.

"Let's take that one." The trailer looked like it was running as fast as it could towards the restroom, couldn't make it in time, and had just decided to try and hide behind some tall weeds on the edge of the forest while it discreetly did its business. Matt started pointing at things on the boat and instructing us in the fine art of boat mechanics.

"Grab that doohickey, wiggle that thingamjiggy, and kick that watchmacallit! It should start without a problem."

Adam clambered over the side of the boat, followed the startup procedure and the boat didn't start.

"Oh, OK. Hmmm… well maybe wiggle the thingamjiggy, grab the doohickey, and then kick the whatchamacallit while pushing the shishkabob." Still nothing. He pondered the situation a bit and had one last go.

"Shake the shishkabob, whack the watchmacallit, pull the dingleberry, kick the thingamajiggy, and shimmey that rattletrap."

The boat still didn't work. At this point the instructions began to include words and phrases that encompassed more than boat mechanics. Matt delved into biology, historical leaders of the Third Reich, and even a little theology. As it turns out, the ignition had filled up with water and was frozen solid. After torching the ignition assembly for ten minutes, all the water drained out of it and the boat roared to life!

Our elation was short lived as we soon discovered another problem. The hydraulic lifters for the prop that drives the boat forward refused to work. This meant that the propeller could not be lowered into the water which meant oars were now more effective than the boat's V8 engine. The issue was that the hydraulic pump was frozen up and so the hydraulic lift system was, to put it in technical boat terms, kaput. Matt thought that maybe, just maybe, the hydraulic system would thaw out by the time we got to the boat ramp and the boat would work. So he decided to take the non-functioning boat along with a smaller, more functioning boat. Matt had traded his old Mallard RV for the smaller boat. I don't know what fine fellow agreed to that trade because the boat was significantly nicer than the rat trap RV. Then again, alcoholism is rampant in Alaska.

Despite being owned previously by an apparent alcoholic, the boat was actually pretty nice. Aluminum hull, huge outboard, light bars, the whole nine yards. Matt had never taken the thing out on water before but he was confident that it was seaworthy.

"It's full of rain water so we know it's watertight," he said. "Besides, we have one or two lifejackets. I think that's them right below the empty gas cans." This boat actually started up without a problem and so we were all set. We hooked the boat up to the van and prepared for our expedition.

My dad has always said that there is a fine line between optimism and stupidity. We should have sensed that maybe we were crossing the line and put fishing off for another day when everything worked. Then again, if we waited until everything worked we may never go fishing again.

The trailer lights didn't work. Matt threw some old towing lights with magnetic bases on the trailer. They didn't work but "At least it looked like we tried," he said. Then we needed fishing licenses. I didn't bother buying any because I was getting pessimistic that we would get out to the inlet. Then we needed to fill up the boat with gas, which took like two hours for some reason. Then the big boat refused to work, again. Then Matt unloaded the smaller boat into the harbor and promptly realized he forgot to put the drain plug in the boat. Luckily the boat was still tied to the trailer so we didn't all drown or die of hypothermia, whichever comes first in Alaska. Once the boat was running and wasn't filling up with water, we all hopped in, excited and refreshed that the boat launch process took a shorter time than it usually does.

We skipped out to our halibut hole in good time. The boat actually performed admirably. Maybe I was stressing for no reason. We were fishing for a good couple hours and were actually having a great time. Then it got dark and cold so we figured we would return to the harbor on the Homer spit. That's when things went south. Actually, they didn't go south, which was the problem because south was literally the direction we needed to go. The boat outboard suddenly started emitting a piercing alarm. Now most people would be overcome with concern when mechanical objects start whining like a two ton bomb hurtling towards its target. I wasn't that concerned because most of Matt's mechanical objects emitted some sort of alarm most of the time. His limo, for example, will randomly produce siren sounds from somewhere in his dash. "That's just letting you know everything is working OK," he says.

This time, however, Matt appeared to get concerned over the siren that was coming from his outboard. This made me a little uncomfortable. Apparently Matt had never heard his boat make that sound before. "Oh man, I think that's the low oil warning." The boat outboard was a two stroke and so it had an oil tank and a gas tank. The oil tank line became broken when someone tap danced on top of it. This caused our entire supply of two stroke oil to be pumped into the bottom of the boat where it didn't do much to lubricate the engine. We were about two miles off the coast and the tide was going in so we didn't have to worry about getting swept out to sea… yet. Unless, of course, we sat here all night and went out with the tide in the morning. In that case we would end up in the ocean where we would probably die or something. I started getting worried. Getting a boat to run when you are in a marina stuffed with twenty tool chests of specialized equipment is still a small miracle. Fixing a boat with a soggy sock, ten numb thumbs, and some rusty pliers while holding a cell phone with your teeth and bobbing around in three foot waves is impossible.

We called my dad who was waiting at the boat dock to inform him we'd be a bit late. "Engine's out, we're trying to get it fixed." Dad knew better than to expect us to get something fixed in the middle of the inlet in the pitch dark. He started worrying too.

We soon found that the engine had a reserve oil tank mounted on the outboard. Giddy with relief, we fired that sucker up and gunned it south, back towards Homer. The light bar was mounted on the rear of the boat, looking forward. It did a great job of lighting up the front of the boat to approximately the lumen output of the sun. The ocean in front of us remained dark and mysterious. This resulted in a herd of clowns all squinting into the night, trying to see past the front of the boat. Luckily for us, we had a marine GPS which had the shoreline mapped on it. We merely watched the dot on the GPS and compared it to the shoreline. I don't have a wide knowledge of sailing but I knew once the dot that marked our spot hit the line that marked the edge of the shore, bad things would happen. Still, it felt irresponsible to not at least look through the windshield and pretend to be able to see where we were going. I would squint into the night and yell directions at Matt, "A little to the left I think!"

Long story short, we made it back – frigid and frozen. We found out that dad was alerting the U.S. Coast Guard to our plight. I would've loved to get picked up by a chopper but Matt seemed somewhat relieved that we got back before it came to that. We consumed our weight in McDonald's burgers then drove home without tail lights. You can take this story and turn it into a plot template for any of Matt's adventures. It's like watching YouTube videos of car wrecks. You know the wreck is coming but you're still surprised how bad it is when it actually happens. Still, I'm always impressed at how Matt refuses to let life become dull. I just wish sometimes he wouldn't feel the need to call me up and ask me to go along. Ha! Who am I kidding? It's about time for another adventure. Matt, call me anytime!

Introduction to Nome
Chapter 1

When we announced our plans to travel to Nome in the early summer of 2016, I was shocked by people's response. The most asked question was: "Nome? Where is Nome? Does that have something to do with gnomes?" This was hardly the rush of hearty enthusiastic congratulations I expected. And no, our book has nothing to do with "gnomes", sorry. I decided it was high time an educational book such as this one was written to inform people about Nome, and the merits of hunting alligators (another common question was "Is it legal to hunt alligators?"). Later folks criticized including an alligator hunting trip in a book about Nome. I do admit a polar bear hunting trip would have been more appropriate, but have you priced polar bear hunts lately? I figure Nome and alligators go together like steak and ice cream. They are very different, but make a great main course and dessert together.

Nome is on the west coast of the Bering Sea. You can't drive to Nome, only fly or take a boat. In the winter you can take a dog sled over frozen rivers to get there. Every year many mushers take part in the Iditarod, the great dog sled race from Anchorage to Nome. That's not to say there are no roads in Nome. There is actually a 300 mile road system connected to Nome. The last great gold rush in America took place in Nome. There are still pieces of mining equipment to be found over the countryside. But I won't say everything here, just read on to find out why *There's No Place Like Nome*!

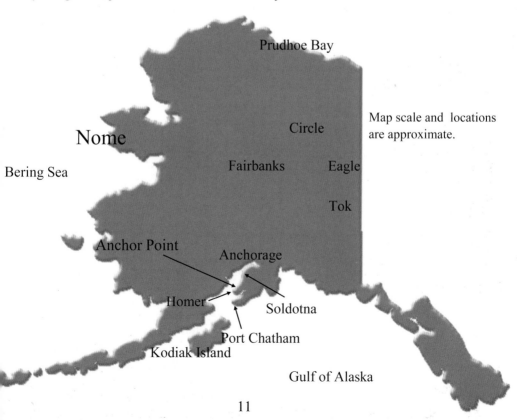

The Nome Gold Rush
Chapter 2

Nome did not exist before 1898. In fact, the name "Nome" comes from a typographical error. Nome is named after Cape Nome, which is close to the present day town. An early navigator put "? Name" on his map, because there was no name. Later someone thought the "?" was a "C" and that "Name" was actually "Nome". Thus everyone started calling this particular section of Alaska "Cape Nome". This just goes to show that typographical errors should be respected as quality literature, capable of changing the future of the country and nation. Just think-if you correct a typographical error, you may be wiping the name of a future town right off the map!

Nome stands as an example of what gold can do to men. In 1989 the "Three Lucky Swedes", Jafet Lindeberg, Erik Lindblom, and John Brynteson left the town of Council to look for a new area to prospect. All the good areas in Council were already claimed, and they didn't want to work for the claim owners. They worked their way up the coast of the Bering Sea and came to Anvil Creek. There they did indeed "strike it rich." They started the Nome Mining District and filed their claims.

In less than one year (12 months), Nome had a population of over 10,000 people! This is a remote spot, in the middle of the wilderness. The closest sea port was in Seattle, over 2,000 miles away! People had to put in some serious effort to just reach Nome, let alone try to live there. It doesn't take a great mind to realize the logistical implications of all these people, thousands of miles away from civilization. Nome has no trees, and is mostly permafrost. It was impossible to dig wells, impossible to dig septic systems. All supplies, including lumber and nails, had to be hauled over 2,000 miles. Buildings put up on permafrost soon started sagging and sitting crooked. The streets turned into mud slogs. In the winter there was no place to go with the waste. This made for some interesting ice formations behind the town's many saloons.

The Nome gold rush single handedly emptied out the Klondike. The gold rush at Dawson Creek, Yukon, had run it's course. Many prospectors were employed by claim owners and worked for wages. When the news of Nome reached Dawson Creek, people left by the thousands towards Nome. Traveling up the frozen Yukon River by dog sled, foot, and even bicycle they headed for Nome. The trip was well over a thousand miles, and nobody knows how many people died along the way. It truly was a stampede, as these rushes are also called.

To make matters worse, Nome had no deep water port. It was literally one of the worst places along the Bering Sea coast to build a city. There was no harbor, and nothing to protect the town from storms sweeping the coast. More than once fires swept through the streets, leveling large portions of the town. Despite all these obstacles, Nome prevailed. The population peaked at 20,000 soon after 1900. For several years it was the largest city in Alaska! Today over 3,000 people still live in Nome.

The Nome gold rush was different than other gold rushes. Typically the way a gold rush worked was like this: Someone would find gold. Thousands more would rush in, but only a few people got claims. The rest showed up after all the claims were filed. They would either then leave, turn to a life of crime, or work for the people that owned the claims. Or in some instances, start a business selling things to the miners. Initially, the Nome gold rush was no different. There was unrest, and legal wrangling and fighting over the claims. Suddenly, someone discovered gold in the sand on the beach! The beach was considered public, and nobody could file claims on it. By 1900 people camped along the beach for 30 miles panning the sands for gold. Nome become known as the "City with the Golden Beaches."

Of course the beach gold didn't last forever. If you pan for gold on the beach today, you're likely to get laughed at. But gold still does get mined today around Nome, commercially and for fun. Nome has come a long way since 1898. It now has a small boat harbor, man made granite wall to protect the town from the sea, and most houses have indoor plumbing. Even today no roads connect Nome to the main road system of the United States. It is still a very unique town, with a distinct Alaskan flavor. It is also lacking "tourist traps" making it an excellent destination for you and your family.

Above: Tents flood the beaches of Nome. You can see the various sluice contraptions setup on the beach. Below: Prospectors work the beach sand. Both photos public domain from Wikipedia.

Nome 1925: Diphtheria Outbreak: Dog Sled Teams to the Rescue!
Chapter 3

"We are prisoners in a jail of ice and snow. The last boat may be justifiably considered to have gone and this little community is left to it's own resources, alone with the storms, alone with the darkness and chill of the North"
-Nome Chronicle

Nome is probably the most famous for the dog sled Diphtheria Anti-Toxin Run of 1925. People who recall the dog sled run often think of the name *Balto*. And yes, Balto was the lead dog for the last leg of the race. However, there were 150 dogs involved, and another lead dog named Togo that was just as, or more important than Balto. There was a total of twenty mushers that took part in this extraordinary run. Not that there is anything unusual about a ground delivery to Nome via dog sled. U.S. Mail was routinely delivered on a dog sled. The difference is this route normally took 25 days to run, but was shortened to just over five days.

Nome is icebound from October to May. In 1925 the only way to get to Nome after freeze up was by dog sled. The airplane was invented in 1903, however the airplanes of 1925 in Alaska were not equipped to fly in arctic winter conditions. They had open cockpits and water cooled engines. Back then antifreeze was not what it is today.

As the last ship left for the season, Dr. Welch, the only physician in Nome for the winter, checked over his inventory. He realized the diphtheria serum that he had ordered the year before had never arrived. The Nome hospital only had serum for several people, and it was expired. Typically, this would be no problem.

Diphtheria attacks the throat, and is spread through air and physical contact. Before the antitoxin was developed, it was a dreaded disease that could wreak havoc on a population and had an almost 100% death rate. It usually attacked children, ages one through ten. The diphtheria bacteria could live for days on a door knob or window sill, and could be spread by people who were not even showing symptoms.

The symptoms of diphtheria can be mistaken for tonsillitis. That December Dr. Welch noted what seemed to be an increase in tonsillitis in town. He was concerned, but not overly worried. On December 24, he was called on to visit an Eskimo/Norwegian girl named Margaret Solvey Eide.

That evening the entire town turned out for the Christmas eve celebration at the town hall. Christmas was a big deal in Nome, as everybody was glad for an excuse to get out and socialize. At midnight the bells of St. Joseph's rang out, and everyone headed to the church for a service.

Normally, celebrations are a positive experience and getting together for a social event is harmless and helps prevent cabin fever. Of course, going to church is even better. This year, everyone would have been better off staying at home, as people unwittingly took Diphtheria with them to the celebrations and spread it around.

On December 28, Dr. Welch received notice that the little girl, Margaret, had died. Tonsillitis is not normally fatal. This concerned Dr. Welch greatly, as he was beginning to suspect he had a bigger problem on his hands than he first thought, but he still was not sure. In January, two more children died. His suspicion grew even stronger that diphtheria might be the cause.

Then, on January 20, his worst fear was confirmed. A three year old boy named Billy Barnett, had been admitted to the hospital a few days earlier. He had a sore throat and swollen glands. As Dr. Welch was making his rounds, he examined Billy and saw the textbook signs of diphtheria. Diphtheria can sometimes be a challenge to diagnose; the earlier victims did not have clear cut signs of the disease .

The next morning Dr. Welch was confronted with more cases of the disease, and by evening it had claimed more lives. The town council was called together, and Dr. Welch laid out the problem. He had 80,000 units of the diphtheria antitoxin on hand, and it was already six years old. This supply, if it was still effective, was only enough to treat six people. He needed one million units to combat the epidemic that was in the process of unfolding.

Seven years earlier the influenza virus had invaded Nome, and over 1,000 people died in the epidemic. The town council had experienced first hand the deadly effects of disease, and an immediate total quarantine was issued. The town went into lock down. Travel was forbidden for children, and discouraged for everyone else.

Telegrams were sent out to the rest of Alaska alerting the state to the need for antitoxin. Nome's epidemic was soon to be front page news across all of America. It was literally a race against time. On the fourth day of the crisis Dr. Welch treated the school superintendent for diphtheria. This was bad, it meant that the entire school had been exposed to the disease.

Over a million units were located on the west coast, but it would be another 10 days until they could arrive by boat to Seward, Alaska. Then a fortunate discovery was made in Anchorage. A Dr. John Beeson found 300,000 units of the serum at the Anchorage Railroad Hospital. This was not enough to stem the epidemic, but it was enough to hold it at bay until the other units arrived.

The next issue was how to get the antitoxin from Anchorage to Nome. The closest railroad ran to Nenana, which was normally a 25 day dog-sled ride to Nome. But many lives would have been claimed by then; it needed to arrive sooner. Airplanes were fairly new to Alaska, and the only experienced pilots were in the lower 48, on vacation. The only plane available was an open cockpit, and the pilot available was inexperienced. Not only was it dangerous for the pilot, if the plane crashed the only available antitoxin within 2,000 miles would go down with it. Ultimately, the airplane was ruled out, and the decision was made to go ahead by dogsled. Even by dog sled there was a risk of something happening to the serum.

The decision was made to use relays of dog teams, instead of using one or two teams for the entire route. The relays would run night and day. Bill Shannon was the first musher in the journey, leaving Nenana with the antitoxin. The serum was packed in a padded box, and weighed 20 pounds. The mushers were supposed to warm it for 15 minutes at every stop to keep it from freezing on the trail.

Bill Shannon ran through severe cold. It was so cold he had to drop off three dogs ailing from frostbite off at Johnny Campbell's roadhouse. It was -62 degrees F actual temperature when he arrived there at 3:00 A.M. After some coffee and a four hour warm up he was on the trail again. The three dogs he dropped off did not make it; they later died. If Alaskan Huskies are dying from frostbite, you know it's cold out. The dog teams kept running, and the badly needed medicine kept heading west.

Henry Ivanoff's team and Leonhard Seppala crossed paths and almost missed each other, due to blizzard conditions. Henry shouted at Seppala, "The serum! The serum! I have it here!"

Seppala was carrying the antitoxin when the weather started to turn for the worse. The blizzard grew so bad Seppala couldn't see his lead dogs on the dog team, and with the wind chill the temperature was a brutal -85 degrees Fahrenheit. Then something happened that made matters get even worse. Seppala had to decide if he wanted to cross the Norton Sound, which was frozen over, or take an extra day and go around it. Knowing that lives were on the line, and he himself had an eight year old child in Nome; he decided to take the quicker, riskier route. As Seppala raced across the ice, the floe started to break away from the main ice on the shore. Togo, demonstrating almost human intelligence, swam across the growing divide. Seppala threw a line over, and Togo pulled the ice floes together, and the team continued on.

Gunnar Kaasen was the last musher in the relay. He was supposed to hand off the serum to Ed Rohn at Point Safety. However, when he arrived the weather was clearing and his dogs were still running strong. His team was led by the famous dog "Balto." Rohn was sleeping when Kassen arrived, so he pushed on the last 25 miles to Nome. He arrived on February 2, reaching front street at 5:30 A.M. Together the teams had run 674 miles in 127.5 hours, in terrible conditions almost the entire distance. This was considered a world record.

Later a second run was made with more serum. The first batch was not enough. However, the first batch had alleviated the crisis. The second batch arrived on February 15, and this was sufficient to stave off the remainder of the epidemic. They did attempt to use airplanes in the second run, but the planes broke down before getting off the ground.

The Nome run made the headlines of national papers, and the mushers became famous. This did cause some problems, as the papers tended to put all the focus on "Balto" and Kaasen, and neglected the other teams. One musher, Charlie Evans, even harnessed himself to the sled when several of his dogs succumbed to frostbite. In reality all the mushers made sacrifices and took great risks, with many of them getting frostbite. Seppala and Togo made significant contributions which did not receive as much attention, causing Seppala to label Balto "the newspaper dog."

One notable event in the serum run: The governor of Alaska actually ordered it stopped because of the terrible weather. However, due to miscommunications the mushers never received this message, and pressed on through whiteout conditions, at temperatures much colder than your ice cream freezer.

Wilma Williams (author of *Alaska Sea Escapes*) has talked first hand to some of these brave mushers. The passage of time has taken them all. She said they tended to be quiet men, and it was actually hard to pry information from them about the run. They just did "what had to be done."

Unfortunately, I do not have the space to discuss each musher's contribution to the serum run. This account has been greatly abbreviated. Entire books have been written about this run. If you are interested in further reading I recommend *The Cruelest Miles: The Heroic Story of Dogs and Men in a Race Against an Epidemic* by Gay Salisbury and Laney Salisbury.

Above left: Illustration of Leonhard Seppala with some sled dogs. Above Right: Gunnar Kaasen with Balto. Below: The 1925 serum route to Nome. Map and above right photo courtesy of Wikipedia, public domain.

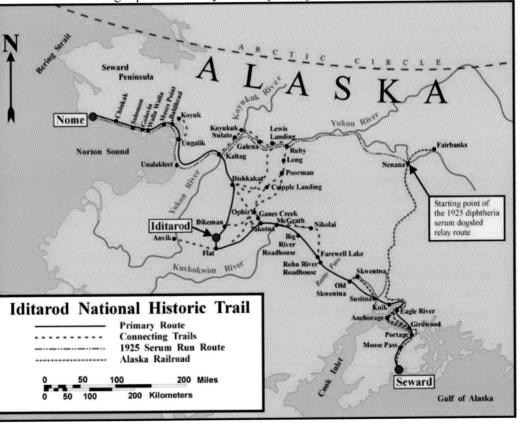

Boat Problems
Chapter 4

A few folks have asked me about the 27 foot boat I hauled up to Alaska last year. What had become of it? I have been silent on this issue for a number of reasons. The first reason is because when our third book was written, it was the middle of February. The boat was sitting safely at my place, not leaving a trail of soggy $100 bills in it's wake. It's pretty boring to write about a frozen boat covered in snow.

Then Marlene's cookbook came along. I helped her with that, and made suggestions about it for content. Wanting the cookbook to be generally positive in nature, I didn't even want her to mention what she thought about some of my boat projects. I'm also fairly certain she wasn't interested in publishing boat stories, unless they concluded with the boats going up in flames. So, here is the boat story.

In the spring of 2016, we took the boat down to the boat shop in Homer, Alaska. This is the same shop where I bought parts for the boat last fall. The people at the boat shop are intelligent, but they don't work cheap. Nor should they. It is obvious they charge a fair rate because they are always busy. The only thing this tells me is there must be a lot of lawyers and doctors in Homer, maybe even politicians. Or, possibly drug cartels, as I don't know who else could afford these market rates.

I like buying old stuff cheap, as some folks may have noticed. However some times it is a challenge to get something cheap and keep using it for cheap. This boat is a classic example of a good deal going bad. After hearing stories of some of my friends having to get towed in off the water, and getting towing bills of a couple thousand dollars, I decided to have the boat shop go over the boat. It also had that annoying habit of not going into reverse, as described in Book 3. I figured a quick tune up job and that linkage repair couldn't be a big deal, maybe $200 or so.

A few days after dropping the boat off, the guy at the boat shop called me. "Your boat engine knocks like..." and then he made comparisons that are not fit to print. This was bad news. When I had winterized it last fall, it had run fine, except for it's tendency to not go into reverse. Wow, this sure wasn't what I wanted to hear. "How could that have happened?" I asked. "Last fall it ran fine." At first I was suspicious the boat shop was just trying to rip me off. But that was not the case.

As you may recall, last fall I had trouble with getting water in the oil. This is a big problem, and in a car engine it means really bad things, like a cracked block or head. In this case, it was actually the water jacket around the exhaust manifold. Car engines do not have water jackets on the exhaust manifold. The manifold was letting water run into the engine, and I fixed it with a new manifold. I changed oil several times, and put the boat away for the winter. But—this is not sufficient for getting water out of an engine, I found out.

To properly clean all the water out of an engine, you must either: 1. Run it several hours to thoroughly warm it up, causing all the water to evaporate out of the crankcase. 2. Fill the crankcase full to the top with either diesel fuel or kerosene. This forces the water off the walls of the block. If you only change oil, water condensation remains on the heads, piston walls, and other engine surfaces. Left alone, these surfaces will happily rust to pieces and cause unhappy thoughts on your part when you start, or try to start the engine again.

I had hauled a boat the whole way across North America, only to destroy the engine. That is not smart. This thought ran through my mind about two thousand, three hundred times after discovering this fact. I asked Lee, the mechanic, to get me a quote on a new engine. I was not about to just dump this boat in the weeds after all the pain I went through to get it there.

What I failed to consider is that a boat without an engine has many potential uses. I could have cut a hole in the side, and used it for a dog house. Or turned it upside down, and built a cabin under it. Or it could be used as a giant bathtub. Instead, I chose the worst option-fixing it.

A few days later, Lee called me up. "Hey, we can't find any new engines for that year of boat," he said. This was a let down. But he had some more ideas. "I can get some quotes on a nifty, new fuel-injected engine, with a lot more horsepower." I like power, and I'm always a sucker for trinkets, so I said, "Sure, go ahead and get me a price." Some more days went by, and I just figured Lee was busy with other projects, it didn't occur to me that it might actually take several days to calculate how much this thing would cost. Finally, Lee called me again. He went on and on about all the wonderful features of this new engine, how it would save fuel, practically cut fuel costs in half, and so on. It even had some kind of way to hook it up to your phone so the mechanics could remotely troubleshoot it. At that point, I began to get nervous. There was no way that kind of setup could be cheap. Finally, he came out with the price.

"You're, ah looking at about $21,000," Lee said.

The world spun, and I staggered, looking for something to steady myself. "Ah, ah, don't touch it right now!" I blurted out, afraid that he might have started on it already, buying some nonrefundable alloy bolts that cost $500 each, which probably were also used on F-16 jets. By my gasping and panting, Lee seemed to deduce that I didn't really want to abandon any hope of ever retiring for the sake of this boat. "Let me think about it a few days," I said, wanting to get off the phone before my rising blood pressure forced me into unconsciousness.

The "let me think about it" was just a ruse to get off the phone. I didn't really need to think much about spending $21,000 on a boat I bought for $2,999. Besides, I knew the drill: If you decide to spend $21,000 the total bill would be $30,000 before you knew what happened. Larry Burkett, the financial adviser who compared boats to fiscally irresponsible black holes, was indeed a genius. Although I did hear him, one time, tell a guy he should think about keeping his boat. They must have had a gas leak in the studio that day.

After I calmed down, a few days later, I called Lee back. "I guess we'll just have to put her out to pasture for good," I said. Then Lee suggested having the boat engine rebuilt by a local machine shop. "That would run about $3,000," he suggested. Uh oh. In hindsight, I was falling for a sales tactic. After the mind blowing, cerebrum short circuiting amount of $21,000--$3,000 sounded like a quick trip for snacks to the discount grocery store. I did some mental calculations. "Hmm, $2,999 for the boat, and $3,000 for the engine, that puts us at $5,999. I can easily sell it for more than that. Right now it's basically worth the same amount as an oversize, wore out bathtub." I decided to go ahead and have the boat engine rebuilt.

One small positive note was that my boat engine was based on a Chevy small block 350. A marine engine is built heavier than a car engine, however the basics are the same. The result is parts and repairs are cheaper than outboard engines. I don't even want to think about the cost of outboard engine repairs. I'm guessing the outboard guys just take their boat out in the middle of the inlet, pull the plug, swim to shore and file an insurance claim (this is illegal and not recommended).

After a good deal of time, the boat engine had been rebuilt. Then I talked to Lee again. He said "Hey, don't you want to put a heater in this boat? A good heater costs around $500." Hmm, come to think of it, every time I go fishing I get really cold. I reasoned a good heater would help the resell value, and if nothing else, help it sell quicker. In hindsight, this was a bad idea. Heaters need to be installed and hooked up. At five thousand dollars an hour, or whatever they charged, even a cheap heater becomes expensive.

Finally, the boat was finished, and put back together. Then I got the bill for the balance of the repairs (I had already paid for the engine rebuild). Let's just say that was a bad day. While it did cost less than $21,000 it was not nearly as much less as I had hoped. I still hope to retire someday, about the same day I turn 100 years old. This is, of course, assuming I never use the boat or buy another one. I have heard "retirement" is a non Biblical idea anyway, so maybe it's for the best.

The *Sergeant* Comes Home
Chapter 5

I need to relate a story that may make people get emotional. At least it seemed to have that effect on Marlene. This marvelous event came about on Christmas, 2015. We were at my parent's place, and it was a family get together. My uncle John was there. If you recall, reading book 3, I had been given the use of a boat for the summer. This was back when I was 18 or 19. My uncle John let me use his boat, the *Sergeant*, for the summer. A 19 foot 1960 Glaspar, it was actually named the "*Delaware Air National Guard Sergeant*", but the first four words were shortened into an acronym on the boat hull. This caused some confusion at times, and frequently I had to explain the boat name wasn't actually a swear word.

So, back to the get together. We were all sitting around enjoying some snacks and discussing Alaska. Most folks mistakenly think that one day I leapt off my chair, grabbed Marlene and the children, and roared off to Alaska. The truth is going to Alaska seems to be a family tradition. My uncle John, aunt Doris, and my grandmother all had spent time in Alaska. My uncle John and aunt Doris had even driven the Alcan highway in the 1980's. That was when it was a real trip. Today the road is a super highway compared to thirty years ago.

Suddenly my uncle John said, "Hey, if you want the *Sergeant* you can have it for free." Wow! I couldn't believe my ears. What a Christmas present! Then John said "Well, maybe you could pay me $500 for the trailer." I didn't hesitate, and promptly agreed to this generous deal. I stole a glance at Marlene, and she was doing her best to conceal her enthusiasm with a grimace.

"Oh, that boat!" my aunt commented. "I remember going out to Raystown Lake, and we always ended up rowing it back!" I appreciated her attempt at injecting humor into the conversation. My dad decided it was his turn for comedy. "I hope you're not taking that boat onto Cook Inlet. It would probably break in half," he said. Laugher echoed across the room. Another person made a comment about the boat being over fifty years old. Really, the Statue of Liberty is at least that old and nobody talks about tearing it down and throwing it away. Those family reunions were always like that, with people cracking jokes and trying to outdo each other.

My uncle's generous boat gift was contingent on one condition: That I remove it from his property as soon as possible. A modest person, he was probably tired of his neighbors thinking he was wealthy, having a boat and all. He even threw a gas tank in with the deal. I promised my uncle I would keep the *Sergeant* and not sell it for a handsome profit, but that didn't even seem to concern him. I thought it would have seemed unfair to profit from a Christmas gift.

Excited, a few days later I picked the *Sergeant* up. It seemed to have aged considerably since I last saw it, but that was ok. I'm sure it will make an excellent boat on Cook Inlet. I remember my one uncle talking about taking it out on the Chesapeake Bay, back in 1978. The Chesapeake Bay is salt-water, just like Cook Inlet. The *Sergeant* should feel right at home there.

The challenge now is how to get it up to Alaska. It is much smaller than the boat I lugged up last year, but that left a bad taste in my mouth. I'm sure something will work out. Maybe we can even pull it up with the limo.

The *Sergeant*, in all it's glory.

A Mallard Motorhome for $2,500!
Chapter 6

Towards the end of May 2016, I again found myself in an unpleasant place: Pennsylvania. This was a little bit like an unsettling dream I have sometimes, I dream I'm working in a tire shop. In my dream I think, "What! Why I am I here?! I quit here 19 years ago!" and then I wake up with relief. Except this was no dream, I was in Pennsylvania again. It seems Marlene couldn't stand our cabin that winter. I must admit I was a little tired of it too, and we returned (temporarily) to the leeks and garlics of Pennsylvania.

Of course, we were careful not to do anything foolish and jeopardize our Alaskan residency, which demonstrates a clear point. To become a resident of Alaska, you need to meet a defined set of requirements (which we have met). You can be there 10 years and not be considered a resident, if you don't take the proper steps to become one. Pennsylvania is different. If you're there too long, wham! Down come the cuffs. You're a resident even if you don't want to be one. The difference is striking. It reminds me of the old East and West Germany. Pennsylvanians themselves will reinforce this, by their own words.

We drive back and forth between Alaska and Pennsylvania quite a bit, for a variety of reasons. Office meetings, family reunions, book signing, etc. In the last few years we have logged well over 50,000 miles driving back and forth between PA and AK. I'm not trying to be pompous, but I am heavily involved and a share holder in five different companies based in Ohio, Alaska and Pennsylvania. Before you're impressed, anyone can file LLC incorporation papers for about $150.

This causes a few misunderstandings. For example, someone might meet me in March at the store. If they happen to see me 6 months later, again in Pennsylvania, they gasp. "What! You're still in Pennsylvania!" they shriek. Then they give out a shrill laugh, similar to what an angry chimpanzee on helium would sound like. As I walk away, they will shriek, "You're no Alaskan-your a Pennsylvanian!" followed by peals of maniacal laughter ringing off the store walls. This is very unsettling, so much so that I have considered ordering groceries online and having them mailed to me.

Let's dissect this "discussion" if you will. First, the shrieking hysterical person assumed that because they saw me twice, several months apart, I had been in Pennsylvania the entire time. That is not logical. If I happen to meet them say, in the store's bathroom, several months apart, they wouldn't conclude I was in that bathroom the entire time. For example, last year I was in at least 10 different states and four different Canadian provinces multiple times.

Yes, I own land in Pennsylvania. But does owning land make me a resident? I own over 13 times as much land in Alaska as I do in PA. And that last accusation, which sends cold shudders down my spine: "You're not an Alaskan..." What if they had said, "You're not an ax murderer," or "you're not a wild-eyed lunatic." In order for the phrase "You're not an Alaskan" to have any kind of merit as an insult, Alaska must be superior to Pennsylvania. But I digress. Enough ranting about this. If you call yourself a Pennsylvanian, I won't insult you. It is ok if you want to live in Pennsylvania.

Another reason we had returned to the shadow land was to send Shane to camp. It, of course, sounds completely insane for an Alaskan to drive to Pennsylvania to go to camp, but that is how it happened.

Our return to Alaska was scheduled to coincide with Shane's last day of camp. We planned to pick him up, and head north. Enough time wasted outside of Alaska.

People often ask how we can afford to drive back and forth between Alaska and Pennsylvania so much, and the answer is simple: We figure out how to make money on these trips. For example, in Book 2, *Return to Alaska*, we hauled a trailer up to Alaska and cleared a few thousand dollars. In Book 3, *The Year of Much Fishing*, we hauled a 28 foot boat to Alaska, and cleared nothing. In fact, the boat, true to boat form, soaked money up the whole way to Alaska, and is still up there soaking up money like a sponge. A tip: Don't drag boats to Alaska. In fact, stay far away from boats. The fact I can keep working while we travel helps immensely. Since all my work is done on a computer, I can do it while we travel.

After doing some research, I discovered motorhomes appeared to sell for more money in Alaska. This was good, because motorhomes are an excellent way to travel. Having lost out on the boat, I decided that I would need to maximize my potential with the motorhome. In other words, I needed to find the cheapest one possible. This led to some unexpected issues later on, but that's for another chapter.

As the month of May was winding down, I still had not found a cheap motorhome. This was fairly concerning, because our other option was to fly home, which would cost several thousand dollars (I didn't have enough air miles on my credit card) and give us no way to recoup the lost money. Finally, one Friday evening I spotted what looked like a winner on craigslist, a 1990 Mallard for $2,500. I had never heard of a Mallard before, but it appeared to be built on a Chevy chassis so I figured it couldn't be too bad. My motto is "strike while the iron is hot" so I immediately set out to secure the RV. I called several times, and the lady answering the phone kept getting me

At first glance, the old Mallard seemed to be stoutly built and in good condition. The previous owners put tape around the windows, which didn't do any favors for the appearance.

mixed up with other people. She was either a very clever salesperson, or else she was getting lots of calls about the motorhome. I wasted no time in setting up an appointment for the next morning to see the vehicle, which was about an hour and a half drive away.

Marlene and the children did not take kindly to me rustling them out of bed early Saturday morning, but we had a deal to catch. We rolled into the motorhome guy's place around 8:30 AM. I soon learned the sellers were not expert salespeople, or so it appeared. The RV had a flat tire, and looked like it was sitting at one place for a long time. "The tires are all shot" they told me. "Better plan on buying 6 new tires." This was good, typically someone selling an RV will emphatically say up and down "The tires are great, just look at that tread!", while dry rot cracks half an inch each deep are all over the sidewalls.

Mike, the guy selling the RV, gave me a brief tour of it. The onboard generator fired right up, which was a good thing. Mike pointed to some stains on the ceiling, and said "The roof used to leak, but it is now fixed." I should have pushed around on the roof a bit more, but it seemed solid at the time. The refrigerator looked new, and actually turned out to work good. So, I told Mike I would buy the motorhome. He did look a bit surprised when I mentioned I was planning to drive it to Alaska. On the way to the notary, someone called Mike and told him "They were at his place to buy the motorhome." He told them "it was sold," and after a great deal of expression by verbal frustration they hung up. I felt smug about snatching up this good buy.

After doing the title work, I went about changing the tire. The spare tire looked great when I pulled the cover off of it. Mike saw this and commented he "should have charged more," but I already had the paperwork done. As I was working on changing the tire, a lady walked up and asked if I was Mike. I replied I was not. She then stated she was here to buy the motorhome, and expressed disappointment when I told her I had just bought it. In hindsight I should have driven back to the notary and sold it to her. Some of the other tires did look a little sickly, and I was worried about driving back the 100 or some miles to our lodging accommodations. But, as usual, I had wasted my time worrying about non-issues. I do tend to worry a lot about silly things.

A few days later we took the motorhome into my parents place to show it off. I had described the motorhome to my dad over the phone, and he wanted to see the bargain of the century. He even said that he might consider buying the fine specimen of an RV from me. Mysteriously though, as soon as we showed up he had a change of heart and didn't want anything to do with it. He did point out some minor flaws in the back, where the side walls met the back walls. It seemed they were starting to separate, and my dad made the outrageous suggestion the motorhome might fall in half if we didn't address the issue. Not wanting to offend his sensitive nature, I suggested if he was worried about this, possibly he could fix it, as he used to work at a camper factory years ago. After I pointed out that I was planning to haul his grandchildren to Alaska in the RV, he obliged to try to fix it.

With this settled, I left the motorhome at his place for repairs. Later, my mom reported that Dad said to her, "This is going to take a lot of work." He then asked her if he should "fix it right," and she replied, "What would Matt do?" When I picked the motorhome up again, it had been "repaired" with what looked like duct tape!

After getting the "repaired" motorhome back from my dad, I had Arlan (from Clark Hill Service Center) go over the mechanical side of the RV and change the transmission fluid, etc. We also decided to only change three of the tires, as some of them appeared quite good. On the way back from Arlin's, the front piece of tin that goes around the front overhang came down, working like a sun visor. This did worry me a bit, as tin shouldn't just come loose like that.

Closer inspection revealed that the wood frame over the front driver's and passenger seat appeared to be rotten and falling apart. I tried running longer screws into the wood, but they just pulled out too. I took a hammer and knocked on the side, and the results were concerning. The plywood inside fell out in rotten looking hunks.

Being one of those types of guys that obsesses over details, I decided to pull out the rotten plywood and replace it. This repair turned into a rather lengthy process that consumed several days. I was pleased with the results though. The rot had not extended to the entire frame, so I was able to leave the basic frame intact and just reinforce it. The floor (or roof, depending on your point of view) over the front driver and passenger seats I replaced with new plywood. Then I applied liberal amounts of caulk to everything and screwed the tin back in place.

A week or two later, Paul asked to borrow the RV for a family camping trip. He had his own RV, which you can read about in Book 3, however, for whatever reason he didn't want to use it. I think it may have had something to do with the fact that it didn't start, or the transmission was acting up. That is why I paid $2,500 for an RV. He only paid $800 for his, and I prefer quality over sub standard motorhomes.

I discovered a little about Paul's character. He seems to be a bit of a whiner. He called me that weekend and said, "It's raining buckets, and it's pouring in through the roof all over the bed." Like I can really control the weather. He also complained about the plumbing leaking, and various other ailments. Later I got Paul to fix the RV, since he seemed to be an expert at finding problems. All he needed to do was throw a sheet or two of plywood on the roof for some extra support and whatnot.

Paul's negative attitude towards the motorhome persisted, despite his repairs, and he even made statements like, "I can't believe you're going to drive this to Alaska!" I laughingly brushed off these comments, but Marlene started getting nervous. "Paul might know what he is talking about," she said. "Maybe you should put that motorhome up for sale on craigslist." I begrudgingly did, but I decided to list it for $6,000 because I did put some new tires on, and my dad and Paul had done their quality work on it.

I guess time would tell if the motorhome was suitable or not. If the RV did sell, our plan was to frantically buy another one off of craigslist for the drive back to Alaska.

I think the limo looks good pulling the *Sergeant*.

Crashing a Drone
Chapter 7

Our pictures seem to be the most popular part of our books. Some might take that data to suggest my writing is sub-par; however, I take it as an obvious compliment to my photography skills (although this wouldn't explain the advice given to me by "real" photographers), or perhaps the magnificence of Alaska. Either way, people wanted more pictures and lots of them. Because of this, we decided to take a family friend, Melissa Sauder, or "Missy" along on part of our adventure. Missy is a professional photographer, and you will see quite a bit of her work in this book. Her sister, Erica, worked for our company, Online Advertising (also known as LancasterPuppies.com), a few years ago. Erica has since moved to Texas, which is almost as good as Alaska.

One day Missy emailed us and mentioned we should have a drone for taking pictures in Alaska. I certainly couldn't disagree, but there is a long list of things I should have for Alaska. Six wheeled AWD side by side, airplane, bigger rifle, a team of champion sled dogs, and one of those 15 passenger all wheel drive Mercedes vans with a diesel (having a large family changes the things you wish for). I'm not trying to get caught up in materialism, just pointing out that there are many things that are handy in Alaska. She was right. A drone would be great for taking pictures, but they are fairly expensive.

A day or two later, Missy emailed again, this time with pictures of a drone and said she bought one! This was an unexpected development. Since she didn't know how to fly her drone, she brought it over for me to try out. Previously I had disclosed that I was a drone pilot. Her drone is a Phantom 3. I had actually flown one of these before, for about three minutes, under the watchful eye of someone who knew what they were doing.

It was dark out, so I decided to just fly the drone in the cabin's living room. I figured I would hover a little bit and experiment with the drone's onboard camera. The Phantom 3 connects wirelessly to a smart phone and provides a live video feed as you fly. The video feed also provides your air speed, altitude, and has an onboard GPS that shows the location on Google maps. The drone can reach speeds of 35 mph, fly up to a mile away from the controller, and stay up for 20 minutes with one charge. Federal law prohibits flying higher than 400 feet. It is a very, very neat piece of machinery. In fact, I hope none of my neighbors have one, as it would make spying on me very easy.

Getting drone flying lessons from Leon Beachy. On the left is Makayla Weaver, and on the right is Paul Weaver. Andy Stoltzfus is towards the bottom right.

The drone setup took awhile, as I had never actually walked through the process myself. I needed to install the drone software on my phone, get the phone communicating with the drone controller, and so on. Finally we were ready to fly. I pressed the controller stick "up" and nothing happened. After more poking and prodding, I remembered there was a button on the phone software to launch it. It was supposed to fly four feet in the air, and hover. I'm not sure what went wrong, but it definitely didn't follow this procedure.

Instead of hovering, the drone flew straight up like a rocket. My brain realized something was going wrong right away, as the drone passed the four feet mark and showed no signs of stopping. I frantically hit the "down" stick on the controller, just as the drone made contact with the ceiling fan, which fortunately was not on. I inadvertently pressed the side control stick at the same time, and after the drone nipped the ceiling fan, it went full speed into the wall. There was a bang, the battery flew out (the drone ejects the battery if it senses something going amiss), and the whole works crashed to the floor. Not on the carpet either, but on the bricks surrounding the wood stove (of course).

Then it was deathly quiet. Marlene appeared a bit agitated. It looked like I may be buying a drone after all. I quickly walked over and checked the drone out. One of the propellers was broken, but otherwise the drone seemed ok. These things are pretty tough, and actually come with spare propellers. After some more checking, the drone seemed fine. A tip for everyone: Don't ever fly your drone in the house!

A later consultation with a friend who has a drone revealed the problem was probably with the GPS positioning. The GPS will not work indoors, and if the drone does not have a GPS signal it will rely on the operator for everything. In this case the operator didn't know what he was doing.

Shockingly, Missy left the drone at our place, as she didn't know how to fly it either. Later I practiced flying it without crashing it. Some flights without crashes bolstered my confidence, and my brother-in-law Mike invited me over to take some pictures with the drone of his new chicken houses. His farm was ideal drone flying territory. However, I discovered there were perils there as well.

Marlene and her sisters were taking a walk, and I figured this would be a good time to test out the drone. You can't really spy on anyone with the drone, as it sounds like a swarm of loud angry bees. As the ladies strolled along Mike's lane, which ran along some trees, I followed them with the drone. My actual location was about 400 feet away on the other side of the trees. One big problem with drone flying is you have no depth perception. It is very hard to tell how far away things like tree branches actually are. Suddenly, a branch flashed on the drone video feed, and then I was looking straight up in the air. The drone video feed will never point straight up in the air, unless something really bad is going on. This was confirmed when the video feed went blank a second later.

Marlene said they were a little surprised when the drone hit a branch and fell out of the sky. Thankfully it didn't land on anybody. The drone is very light, but it is still heavy enough that you don't want to bonk people on the head with it.

Fortunately, the drone still worked, but this crash was harder on it than the crash in my living room. It bent the one arm a little bit, but not bad enough to interfere with its function. I changed batteries and launched it again, and it flew fine. What a relief!

I don't think Marlene likes the drone. She doesn't even like shooting guns, but the one day she mentioned it would be fun to try to shoot it out of the air with a shotgun. On another occasion someone gave me an article about a person who got a drone, but ended up crashing it in a swimming pool. The author's wife, fully clothed, jumped into the pool in an attempt to rescue the drone. When Marlene read the article, I asked her if she would go to such efforts to rescue a drone. Marlene's response was that she would throw the drone into the pool! I wonder if they make waterproof, bullet proof drones….

I even took a picture of the Mallard with the drone! Taken in Anchor Point, AK.

Shopping for a Dogsled Team
Chapter 8

I have always wanted to have my own dog sled team, although it was pretty low on the list for a long time. Then one day I came to the realization that I was running a classified website (LancasterPuppies.com) with over 3,000 dogs for sale on it. Why on earth wouldn't I have a dog sled team? Suddenly it seemed crazy to not have one.

One misconception with sled dogs is that they are always purebred Alaskan Malamutes or Siberian Huskies. These dogs do pull sleds nicely, but they do not win races. The real race winners are sometimes part Malamute and often part Siberian, but almost never purebred. The real race dogs of the north are called "Alaskan Huskies." This is a fancy name for a mixed breed with a long coat and that can run fast. But don't confuse these mixed breeds with just any mixed breeds. These dogs are bred to run for miles without stopping. They are the champions of the Iditarod and Yukon Quest. The merit of each dog is based on it's performance, and not some scrap of paper connecting it to a breed registry somewhere. I have no problem with breed registries; if you want, say, a Basset Hound, a breed registry is the best way to make sure that is what you actually get. But if you want to race, it's a different story.

I admit at getting annoyed when breed registry judges email us and demand we don't advertise dogs for any competing breed registry because they just are not as good. Yes, this has happened. The idea that a dog just isn't good because it's nostril is out of place or it's ear is crooked seems kind of silly to me. Also, I have not noticed any difference in the major breed registries regarding the quality of purebred dogs. So it is a bit refreshing when papers don't matter. I never was one to like paperwork anyway.

Because we don't have (yet) many advertisers in Alaska, I had to pick some dogs in the lower 48. Just because race dogs are mixed doesn't mean you want to just buy say, a German Shepherd/Lab mix and start running it behind a sled, although that combination might actually work. After some research I decided on the Alaskan Malamute. They are not known for speed, but are easier to train and will pull like small horses. There were a number of Malamutes for sale on LancasterPuppies.com, but two caught my eye. They were six or seven months old, and looked very nice. I decided to pick this pair up. They were both males, and brothers.

We drove the old Mallard to pick the dogs up. I don't remember why, probably because none of the other vehicles would start, or they may have been in storage at Clark Hill. As we drove into the farm, I noticed two enormous dogs wandering around the yard. "I bet those are the parents," I told Marlene. "Look how big they get!" Eager to see the dogs I was going to buy, I got out of the RV and found the seller.

The seller informed me that these huge dogs were actually the six month old dogs I had come to pick up! And they were not yet full grown! She said the parents both were in the 120 pound range, and these dogs would almost surely get that big too.

I had to laugh when I looked at the dog carrier I brought along. Half of one of these dogs wouldn't even fit in it. So we put the dogs right in the motorhome, and brought them back to the cabin that way. We weren't sure what to name the dogs, as the previous owners didn't really have names for them. As we were driving Mary Kate pointed to the dogs and said, "Bears." So the one dog got the name Bear. The other dog we decided to name "Balto" after one of the lead dogs in the Nome serum run of 1925.

I picked up a few more dogs, including a free Siberian Husky from a high school reunion. I don't really like reunions that much. The high school reunion is every five years, and often we are not in Pennsylvania when they occur. The one reunion we missed because we were in China when it happened. Anyway, since this particular reunion happened while we were in PA, we decided to go to it. As I was sitting there chatting with a fellow named Herb Martin, who married Melissa Bowman (who was in my class); I mentioned I was raising some Huskies. Herb perked up and asked if I wanted a free dog. "Free" and "me" belong in the same sentence! We picked up the dog that very night. Her name is Shae, and she was 4 years old. I ran her with the team, and she caught on quickly. While she probably won't ever actually race, it's nice to have extra dogs for the training team and for fun.

We also have two other Siberian Huskies named Toaster and Bonanza. These dogs are small for Huskies, weighing around 45 pounds each. While not working on training the dogs, they are kept at my parents' place. My parents are actually the owners of all the sled dogs, until we transport them to Alaska (which will be soon). The current arrangement is that I keep them at our PA cabin when training them. Since we are in Alaska a lot of the time, they don't get the training like they should, but they are catching on really good anyway. My brother-in-law Paul, who still lives in Pennsylvania, also helps with the dogs. And yes, in case you are wondering, the dogs all are licensed in Pennsylvania. I mention this because I know the dog warden reads my books. :)

Above: Shae in her harness. Below: Balto and Bear in the lead, followed by Bonanza and Shae. Getting dogs to stay in a straight line can be a challenge! I'm using a custom built training scooter, tag lines, and harnesses. It really is a lot of fun!

One weekend I was working on training Toaster and Bonanza, they ran off. This was a serious problem, as I didn't want to lose the dogs in the first place, and all the training was useless if I didn't have the dogs. Frequently in the past I let the dogs run loose, while getting ready the harness or tag line on the training scooter. Before they had always behaved, but not this time. After a few hours they did not return, and I started growing desperate.

It was not until almost two days later I discovered they were at the SPCA (dog shelter) in Lock Haven. On their facebook page they had pictures of Toaster and Bonanza, however it said they were "well behaved." In my opinion they were not well behaved! Somewhere the dog warden picked them up and took them there. Because their dog licenses were not on their collars, they didn't know who owned them. Pennsylvania law does not require the dog license to be on the dog itself if the dog is kept in an enclosure. Because the dogs have a very annoying habit of chewing their collars, we kept the licenses off the dogs. I think I may get them micro chipped.

The SPCA charged me $5 a dog to get the dogs back, plus $11 for boarding. I found this very reasonable, and I was impressed how they handled everything. With that said, I'm still not a wild fan of the SPCA. I had to show ID, and spend 10 minutes explaining why I had an Alaska drivers license, and then describe the dogs before seeing them to prove they were actually ones I lost. But, I guess those are safe guards to prevent people from claiming dogs that are not theirs. To the Lock Haven SPCA and the dog warden who took the dogs there: Thank you! We are very thankful to have the dogs back safe and sound. And, we will try very hard not to have this happen again!

Some of the fellows from A.B. Martin Roofing in Ephrata, PA, drove the limo to the Ark Encounter in Kentucky. While they were gone I received complaints from them about the heater not working, and when the car was returned the sunroof was covered with duct tape! I patiently explained that Alaska limos don't have all the fancy stuff like limos in the lower 48.

Photo by Leroy Martin

The Diesel Rabbit
Chapter 9

In June the days were winding down to our departure date, and the motorhome still had not sold. My brother, Josh and his wife, Janice, had gotten married the year before. Now the rumor is I had promised them an exquisite, all expense (or at least most of it) paid trip to Alaska. The truth is I had only promised plane tickets to Alaska. They were planning to take advantage of this offer and fly into Anchorage in early July. I knew Josh had talked about driving to Alaska several times, and I thought he might appreciate the chance to do so. He confirmed that they would indeed be interested in this opportunity, and as a result, I didn't book plane tickets.

Their vehicle of choice (because it was the only one I offered) was my vintage 1984 diesel Rabbit. There is a bit of a long story behind this particular Rabbit. I had purchased it several years ago for $500 but had not yet gotten around to transporting it to Alaska. I had stored it at Clark Hill Service Center for most of the time I owned it.

A little trick on dealing with garages: if you need a vehicle stored for free, just take it to your local garage with some minor repair, and tell them that you are not in a hurry for it. If they do happen to repair it before you want the car back (which is fairly unusual), tell them you want something else repaired. This works best with rusty old vehicles that actually have a long list of problems you eventually want fixed anyway. In the case of the Rabbit, there were plenty of repairs to go around, but most of them were non essential. If your garage does repair your car quickly, even though you tell them it's "no hurry," it's time to find another garage. They obviously don't have enough work to do.

It is important I insert a quick word here: Arlan (Clark Hill Service Center) will get things done in time, if I ask him to. He has done many 11th hour repairs for me, meaning I drag something into the shop at 11pm and want it back by 11am the next day. Because Arlan is busy dealing with customers hauling cars in late at night and demanding he fix them immediately, repairs that people say "are not a hurry" will wait for a long time.

While in PA, I figured I might as well drive my Rabbit a bit before the big trip. It allegedly get's 50 mpg, and it well may because the whole time I owned it I did not even run one tank of fuel through it. It even crossed my mind to make the employees drive it (they put a lot of miles on), but they threatened to quit when approached with that prospect.

One day, about a week before we planned to leave, while driving the Rabbit I noticed an odd phenomenon. Every time I would make a right hand turn, strange scraping sounds would come from the back of the car. My finely tuned mechanical ear detected a problem with this, so I stopped and looked under the car. It seemed the rear axle was crooked, causing the tire on the one side to scrape the wheel well on turning. I sighed. It seems I always get stuck with the lemons. For example, one time I bought a Ford Tempo for $200, only to have the alternator give out several weeks later.

Arlan does welding, so I figured this axle issue with the car would be an easy fix. I promptly headed over to his shop with the car. After crawling underneath and taking a look, Arlan looked grim. "The axle mount appears to already have been jimmy-rigged once already," he said. I told him I wanted it fixed ASAP, then left with one of my other vehicles that was in storage at the garage. I alerted Josh that we were having complications with the Rabbit, and he did his best to not appear devastated at the news.

The next day Arlan called me, with bad news. "The car is so badly rusted, there is nothing to weld on to," he said. When I told him to try harder, he suggested other welding shops in the area might be better qualified to repair the Rabbit. What horrible news! I hate when garages suggest my cars should go to the junk yard. Actually, now that I think about it, the last time I sold a car was when I was eighteen. The rest all ended up in junk yards, many because of the Pa vehicle inspection racket. The vehicle repair industry is indeed in a sad state of affairs.

Our situation was getting a little desperate. We were supposed to leave shortly on our trip back to Alaska, and Josh and Janice didn't have a ride. Last minute plane tickets are often more expensive. Suddenly I thought of another option: Josh and Janice could ride with us in the motorhome to Alaska! After all, it was 26 (or 27) feet long and had plenty of leg room. I called Josh and offered the proposal they ride with us. I pointed out our children were small, and they would practically be traveling in luxury, with the onboard bathroom, refrigerator, stove, etc. Typical of the younger generation, he seemed more concerned about having an outlet to charge his phone. I assured him the Mallard had a generator. He also carefully counted up the amount of people that would be in the motorhome. "So you have 7 children," he said. "Yes," I replied. "But the small children we can put on the bed. They won't take up much room." After some thought, he replied that it seemed workable, so that's what we should plan on.

Later, I realized I had forgotten to mention there would be additional people along besides our family, but only two. Let me explain. It is a bit lengthy. First, when folks realize you drive back and forth between PA and AK, they assume you want to be a delivery service. Shipping things to Alaska is expensive, and many places are too obstinate to even ship to Alaska.

Also I don't mind taking a few extra items along, and so folks in Alaska will ship things to PA, and I'll take them along up to Alaska with our stuff. This system is not without risk to the recipients.

Several months prior, when Marlin Eicher heard we would be in PA, he asked if I would bring some things along for him if he shipped them to PA. Since Marlin has loaned us vehicles, helped build our cabin, and generally bent over backwards to help us, I, of course, wanted to accommodate him. But I forgot about his request, and a coincidence made the situation worse.

A friend of mine told me how wonderful spray-on grease was. I went online and actually looked into ordering some, and thought I should get two cans of it, but I didn't actually go through with the order. A few days later, two cases of spray-on grease showed up at our PA cabin address. This puzzled me greatly, but I am always busy and forgetful, and I figured I must have ordered grease and got two cases by accident.

With plenty of grease on hand, I went about trying it out. The stuff did work great! I oiled up a 4-wheeler shift linkage, tried it on bike chains, and used it many other places. My friend Shannon was over one day, and I told him how I accidentally ordered two cases of this stuff and he might as well take some. After extolling the virtues of it, he took several cans. I don't normally just hand stuff out, but Shannon is a good friend and has helped me with many projects, so he deserved some.

A few days went by and a bunch of garage door parts showed up! Now I was really confused. I was pretty sure I didn't order garage door hardware. That's not something I just browse for online either. My brother-in-law Harlan, has Rissler Garage Doors, but he never shipped me things like that. Puzzled, I went through the whole box. At the bottom there was a paper that said "Sterling Supply" on it. The lights went on! I realized that Marlin was shipping stuff to me, to take up to him, and instead I was just using it and giving it away!

Another time someone from Pennsylvania wanted me to take a half-grown Rottweiler along to drop off in Fairbanks, in order to save them $500 in shipping. They must have been unfamiliar with geography, because they acted insulted when I wouldn't even consider it. With seven children to take care of, the last thing we need for traveling a week is a half-grown Rottweiler in the van. Not to mention Fairbanks is several hundred miles out of the way! Alaska is huge, after all.

All this to get to our point about having extra people in the motorhome. Someone called and asked me if I would haul their 10-year-old daughter to Alaska. Girls don't generally bark, drool, need walked, and chew up the interior of the vehicle, so I figured we could. I was concerned about the border crossing, because they get really bent out of shape if you show up with extra children in the vehicle that are not yours. However, the destination got changed to Jamestown, North Dakota. It was even right along the route, so this worked out great. The girl's name was Evana, and she was about the same age as Desiree, which helped.

The second person to come along was Missie Sauder, a photographer and family friend. She likes to travel and had been in Alaska before. She was going to travel up with us, then stay with friends (the Calvin Yoder family) in Alaska and then fly back to Pennsylvania.

Ethan Zimmerman and his family at the Kenton Chair Shop.

The events of the late spring/early summer blur together a bit, so I'll just stick them in this chapter. I don't remember if it was before or after I picked up the Malamutes. In the spring of 2016 we had book signings in Ohio and Delaware. But the exact time frames are not important. The Ohio book signing was in Berlin, at the Gospel Bookstore. We decided to drive the limo, as people get a kick out of seeing it.

We were cruising down a highway somewhere in Ohio. I don't even know what the road name was, I was just blindly following the GPS. As we were cruising along, I thought I heard someone yelling. With seven children in the back, hearing yelling is pretty normal. But this seemed like it was coming from outside the car. Glancing over, I was startled to see a guy driving right beside us (this was a four lane highway) and yelling at me. My ears strained, and I heard, "Hey Matt! This is your cousin Jason!" Suddenly I realized that I was actually looking at my cousin, Jason Rissler (no relation to my brother-in-law Harlan Rissler). I had vaguely remembered he had moved to Ohio at some point in the past, and I had probably not seen him for 10 years. Jason made some wild hand motions that I couldn't interpret, followed by more yelling that I couldn't quite make out.

Jason got off at the next exit, and we followed. He pulled over in a parking lot, and I swung in behind him. It turned out we were only a mile or two from Jason's house, and he invited us over. This was one of the very rare times we were early, so we decided to go visit Jason and his family. His wife's name is Heather, and they have several children. Jason is a pastor at a local church in their community.

Somehow, I'm not sure how, we got on the topic of Bigfoot. Jason mentioned Ohio has it's own Bigfoot legends, aka "The Grassman." I was delighted to hear this. Being an ardent biologist (I frequently shoot my specimens in my field research, and the more interesting ones get mounted for further study), I'm always open to researching nature, especially cryptids. For some reason the field of cryptids seems to be full of nutcases, so a few scientifically minded people like myself are needed to give it some respectability. I prefer cryptids (A cryptid is an animal that supposedly doesn't exist but it may be because government hides the evidence), because who in their right mind wants to sit around and discuss boring animals like squirrels or birds. You can just go to a zoo to see them.

The Grassman supposedly hangs out at the Salt Fork State Park area. Oddly, Marlene isn't always enthusiastic about my scientific pursuits, and insisted I forget about the Grassman. When I did a google search on the Grassman, it appeared that various people had already documented it's existence. However, watching their videos quickly reminded me of the need for more serious minded professionals in the field of Bigfoot research. All the researchers appeared grossly overweight, and seemed to care little about firearms safety. Their guns looked so old they probably didn't work anyway. To top it off, the one guy kept falling in a creek! In another video they used very outdated equipment and attempted to pass it off as state of the art. One guy attempted to make a Bigfoot decoy, and nailed it to a tree. Had the decoy attracted any Bigfoots, it would have been proof that they can't see well, or are slightly more intelligent than cucumbers. Less scholarly types would be quick to use this material to cast doubt on the serious minded Bigfoot researchers, which I'm sure are outraged but just haven't gotten around to expressing their feelings. And typical of cryptid videos, the "proof" video was so shaky it almost inspired seasickness and outright nausea. I suppose we should just be happy the video slipped past the government screeners.

Another book signing took place in Delaware at Central Christian School in Dover. We are friends with Nelson and Monica Martin. Nelson is originally from Lancaster, Pennsylvania. He invited us to be part of their annual school fundraiser. It is a little bit like a fair with games and lots of food. We also visited Ethan Zimmerman and his family. The book signing had been planned for some time, and Ethan emailed me telling me how he enjoyed our book. We exchanged a few emails, and then I mentioned to Ethan that we might be in his area (I didn't know where he lived except it was in or close to Maryland). It turns out Nelson lived about two miles from Ethan's business!

Ethan has a woodworking shop and bought a set of books for each of his employees, which I thought was an excellent idea. Later I ordered a kitchen from Ethan for our new house in Alaska. I guess this worked out good for both of us! His business name is Kenton Chair Shop, but they do much more than only make chairs. Don't miss their coupon in the back of the book!

On a side note, Delaware doesn't seem to have any Bigfoot legends except one called *Moth Man*. I suppose he comes out at night and flies around dust to dawn lights or maybe eats old clothes. Don't let the *Moth Man* in your closet! Careful in the woods-he might nibble on your clothes when you're not looking! Ok, that just doesn't seem very scary or exciting. Maybe we'll write the *Moth Man* off as one of those unsubstantiated legends pushed by crackpots.

Home to Alaska in the Mallard (with 13 people)
Chapter 11

Finally, the day to head home arrived. Evana's mother dropped her off around 10 A.M., then we picked up Missy at her house. Finally it was off to camp to get Shane. After we had Shane on board, we headed for Indiana. Josh and Janice lived in Indiana and were only a few miles off the route to Alaska.

We rolled into Josh and Janice's place around 2:00 A.M. They, for some reason that I will never understand, live in town. The only place to park was across the street in a church parking lot. We parked there and slept for the night. It was here that I already noticed some issues with the Mallard's plumbing. When we awoke in the morning, the Mallard was surrounded by a huge wet spot. It was obvious the gray water tank was leaking. The pipe under the sink was also leaking, which meant we needed to turn the water pump off after using it. Of course, nobody seemed to remember this small detail.

Because Josh went to the effort of blogging about this trip, we will turn it over to him. At the end of his blogs I will offer some additional details and fact checks. We did actually arrive in Alaska, despite his rather, uh, negative perspective on the travel experience.

Everyone but Missie is in this picture, taken in Indiana, before leaving Josh's place.

Just North of Normal Part 1: Traveling to Alaska in Third World Style
By Josh Snader

I have a lot of friends who have been all over the world. Thailand, Loas, China, Mexico, Cambodia, Nepal, Grenada, Belize, etc, etc. I too, have been to many of those places. It's great seeing new cultures, getting diarrhea from new food (Thailand), puking every 30 minutes for 48 hours straight from food poisoning (Mexico), or riding the punctual, clean public transit in Hong Kong (A clean and punctual public transportation system should be considered one of the wonders of the world, in my opinion). But getting to these places can be expensive. I have a cheaper solution to relieve that travel itch, however temporary it may be.

Think about it. You spend $1,000 on a plane ticket so you can travel comfortably to the far end of the world. What do you do when you get there? You experience the local culture which means riding tuk-tuks around, traveling in cramped buses full of chickens and goats, sweltering in the heat, using the bathroom in uncomfortable positions (China) and having things go drastically wrong so that you find yourself in awkward and dangerous situations. But all those highlights of travel can be achieved must easier and with less cost.

For example…

My brother gave me and my wife a free round trip to Alaska. Of course, like any generous gifts from my brother, it came with some ulterior motives. He lives (part time) in Alaska and has been trying to get me and my wife to relocate up north. This is an easy sell for me because I already own 9 acres on the Kenai Peninsula which I bought when I was convinced that I wanted to be a hermit in the wilderness 4,000 miles from where I grew up. But then I met the beautiful woman that is now my wife. She just shudders whenever living arrangements in Alaska are discussed.

"Brrrr. Igloos. Snow. Cabin fever. Bears. Death. Ice. Snow. Deaths. Ice. Ice. Ic…" At this point I interrupt her.

"No income tax."

"Yea, because you'll be dead."

It goes on and on in similar fashion. In an effort to get some more neighbors, Matt has arranged the trip knowing that once a person has visited Alaska, hooks get set deep in the heart that draw you back. And therein lies his ulterior motive.

A few months ago, Matt began hedging his generosity a little. "Hey, do you want to drive up to Alaska instead of flying? We're going up in June. You guys can come with us then fly back."

I agreed, a little suspicious of any vehicle Matt gives me to drive. Sure enough, about two weeks before we were slated to leave Matt called me.

"Hey, we can't take the limo because we need it to drive to book signings," Matt explained. Matt had written a self published book about driving his limo to Alaska called "The Adventures of A Traveling Dog Salesman." It is an interesting book although it reads as though it's been proofread by a five-year-old foreign exchange student. Nevertheless, it has made him a local celebrity among the conservative Mennonite population in Pennsylvania. Apparently it doesn't take much to entertain them although I grew up with Matt so maybe the novelty of his exploits escape me. Matt did something that was weird and almost got killed? Meh, what's new? Matt then proposed a solution, "Would you be willing to drive the Rabbit?"

The Rabbit in question was purchased for $500 (which was about $450 too much) and featured a tiny diesel engine miraculously held in place by rust and a lot of zealous prayer on the part of whoever was driving the car. I agreed to drive it, of course. My life can always use more fervent prayer, and I'll put up with a lot to get a free trip to Alaska. I'd ride a donkey if I had to.

Then, three days before the trip I learned that the Rabbit had run into some small mechanical problems. "The rear axle fell off the Rabbit," Matt informed me. "But don't worry, we're welding it back on." As it turned out, the car was so rusty that there was nothing to weld the axle to. So the Rabbit was retired to it's namesake's natural habitat; heavily wooded land with lots of undergrowth.

Since Matt was an avid collector of high mileage used cars that even low balling Craigslist shoppers didn't want, there was no lack of alternatives. We were taking the 27 foot RV. Twenty-seven feet sounds spacious until you realize that Matt has seven children, all each cuter than the last. Cuteness doesn't make up for lack of space however, and after four days the cuteness factor may not be able to counteract the cramped elbows and sticky fingers.

As I write this, I'm sitting at a table tapping away on my iPad. We are going 55 mph down a toll road but judging from the sounds this Mallard RV is making, we're approaching reentry into the atmosphere. It also smells like burning rubber, which believe it or not, loses its appeal after several minutes. The back corners of the RV are covered in silver gasket tape from top to bottom end in an effort to keep water out. Whether the tape actually works is of little consequence because the air conditioner on the roof is making the carpet in the hallway wet. I guess we could just turn it off but it is keeping the inside of the RV at a cool 89 degrees, which is better than the sweltering outside temperature of 92 degrees. Of course, the windows don't seal very well so the breeze helps keep the burning rubber smell to a minimum. Yes, we could open the windows the whole way but then a few kids might get squeezed out. And that wouldn't be good at all. The bathroom is so tiny that when you close the door, the door handle is competing for space with your knees. That's a good thing, however, since you want to keep a steady hand on the door handle because the door has no locking mechanism. I suspect the shower is merely a refrigerator sourced from the local morgue with a hose stuck through the top end.

I don't want to sound ungrateful. I'll take adventure in any form I can find it, and this trip already feels like an epic adventure in a faraway land but we're only a few hours down the toll road. Big budget adventure for an affordable price.

More updates to follow. Stay tuned!

The 1984 Diesel Rabbit that was condemned by the garage. Note the custom rear bumper.

We're somewhere in Minnesota. The trees are all tall and white here. A local told me that they are fans so the cows don't overheat. You learn new things everyday.

Every state I drive through I evaluate whether or not I could ever live there. This is because I love living in different areas of the country. If I find a better state to live in, why not? You get to experience new cultures, new traditions, new scenery, etc. Minnesota I immediately scratched from the list because their state motto is in French. Duh. This is a no go.

The name Minnesota comes from the Native American tribe of Dakota. It means "clear blue water." There's clear blue water in nearly every other state so I don't see the novelty of this. Then again, they didn't have access to pool chemicals, and I assume they also used large bodies of water as toilets so maybe blue water was actually something to be thankful for. I'm not sure.

You may have noticed that history isn't my strong point. Wisconsin was beautiful, however. Lush farmland was a joy to drive through, and as a liberty loving conservative, I love what Scott Walker is doing with the state. I regret that I hyped up the trip so much. Obviously, driving is getting monotonous, and there isn't much happening besides some half hearted games of Yahtzee (of which I won). There's also the chance to jump out at every gas station to see if this state has any new energy drinks that weren't available in the last state. Nothing really to report there either. On an unrelated topic, you shouldn't drink energy drinks at every gas stop when you're stuck in a 27 foot camper.

There was a little bit of excitement when the motor home stopped working. Most of the excitement came from me since I had an opportunity to get outside and walk rapidly around the motor home pretending to be helpful. After opening the hood Matt and I were relieved to see the engine still inside the engine bay. "Well, that's better than some of your vehicles," I said to Matt. He agreed it was a good start.

We checked the oil. There was oil on the dipstick. That's also a good sign. After noticing that the generator had also shut off, we assumed it was the fuel pump (the generator and the engine use the same fuel source). Fuel pumps love to give out in the middle of nowhere, it's their favorite thing to do. They like to die and take as many people with them as they can. In that way, they sort of have a jihadist vibe to them. I crawled under the camper and hit the gas tank repeatedly, giving it a stern lecture. Sometimes if some thing is a little loose in there, hitting it can sort things out. While that method doesn't work so well for stupid people it did actually work for the gas pump, and we were on our way again! Matt, however, taking a lesson from our president, refused to admit the gas pump had terrorist tendencies, waved his hand in the air, and said we'll fix the problem later. So that's fun! I in some hopes of having more material to write about, I'm simply riding along and waiting to see what disasters come next.

Maybe I'll loosen the lug nuts so my next blog post is more interesting. Stay tuned!

We're somewhere just out of Rugby, North Dakota. The huge sky, expansive landscape, and fresh air draw a sharp paradox to the cramped quarters inside the RV which at this point smells like a porta-potty on wheels. You know those porta-potties at the fair where you hold your breath for the duration of your hurried stay? Well in this porta-potty you can't hold your breath because you are traveling down the highway at a breakneck 55 mph for hours on end. I now understand why dogs – who have a even better sense of smell than humans – prefer to stick their heads out of the window. I find myself doing the same thing. I crank open the window just a crack and stick my nose out, inhaling deeply. I would open the window the whole way, but I don't want the wind ripping the window out entirely – a definite possibility in this 1990 Mallard Sub Quality Wagon LX.

Let's back up just a little bit. Yesterday I got the rare pleasure of driving probably the last Mallard RV alive – which I have dubbed the "Lame Duck" – for several hours across the rolling hills of North Dakota. Most other Mallard RV's were burned at the stake in fervent religious services in an effort to eradicate the foul language that frequently accompanied Mallard ownership. It was remarkable then, that I found myself driving such a special vehicle. The joy of such an occasion was wearing thin since the North Dakota cross winds were impressive and incessant.

In lame duck fashion the Mallard would almost lift off, dragging its one lame wheel along the highway. Just as flight was about to be achieved we'd lose favorable wind and all four wheels would hit the ground again with a jolt and a burst of tire smoke, making the driver saw at the wheel in an attempt to straighten the Lame Duck's path. The fun of floating weightless around the inside of an RV for five second intervals soon wears off, both for the driver and the passengers.

Lucky for us, Matt saved the day by forgetting to empty the sewage tank again, which gave us the ballast we needed to get forward traction. I couldn't help but notice signs warning against drunk driving which made me laugh. It's so empty out here that I could get hammered, drive 100 mph in any direction, and hit less things in a week than a sober New Jersey driver hits in a day.

In the evening we were planning on staying at a friends cousin's uncle's in-law's house that my brother's church buddy from a different denomination knew from a mission trip twenty years ago. Or something like that.

It's a Mennonite thing. You wouldn't understand (unless you are the member of an Italian mafia family or other nationally based, tightly knit group of distant relatives). Our expected arrival time was 9 o'clock but we arrived fashionably late at around 11 o'clock that night. Our hosts were gracious and the food tasted amazing. We also had the extraordinary opportunity to use a shower that was bigger than a shoebox and a toilet that wasn't mounted above an axle. It was the highlight of the trip so far.

The next morning we hit the road again and promptly found that the generator wasn't working. We stopped in the middle of the highway to investigate. A nice feature of North Dakota is 1) You can stop in the middle of the highway without even annoying anyone since there isn't anyone around and 2) If there is someone around they will stop and see if you need help. It's classic rural America at it's finest.

After much poking and prodding we discovered someone had turned off the breakers for the camper. When you have so many children stuck in one box, the odds of having an elbow, finger, or knee turn off something necessary goes up.

UPDATE: I found that the vent in the bathroom has a powered computer fan in it. I turned it on. It sounds like a bat being thrown into a meat grinder but it has alleviated some of the funk in the trunk.

We stopped at Glen and Marilyn Slaubaugh's place near Rugby, North Dakota. Glen is pictured above. The day before we dropped Evana off with her brother in Jamestown, North Dakota.

The yellow flowered crops are Canola. These pictures are of Glen's fields. He farms 1,000 acres but would like to buy or lease more acreage, because he said a 1,000 acre farm is small out here. He even asked to borrow money for land from me! I asked if he thought a millionaire would drive a falling apart camper. He said I may have been trying to conceal my wealth… Ok, lets go with that. I wonder what he would have said about the Rabbit.

My previous entry's date was incorrect. It seems my watch's date function doesn't work correctly. I will return it to WalMart, er, the fine local jewelry store upon my return.

The journey is going according to plan. Of course, that doesn't mean much because there is no plan except to keep the wheels rolling in the direction of Alaska. Also, keeping the wheels attached to the RV would be a nice bonus but I don't want to get carried away with crazy expectations.

We crossed into Canada yesterday, at least I think it was yesterday. The days get muddied when you sleep in an RV that is so bouncy you get a concussion every time you let yourself relax. The border patrol folks were really nice but insisted on searching the RV although we assured them that it wasn't worth looking over. They claimed they were looking for guns and illegal substances but I suspect they were more interested in trying to figure out how we got so many people into that little RV without it exploding from the internal pressure. They even got a ladder out and looked on the roof. The search was quick thanks to the toxic fumes leaking from the bathroom, which encouraged the officials to be prompt.

I lost data service right after crossing the border and went into withdrawal. I had to rely on the knowledge stored offline in my brain to function. No longer were questions like "Where is Canada?" or "Should I pet large, carnivorous wild animals?" easily or quickly answered by technology. Instead I had to actually search my brain for knowledge I learned in the past. My brain opens up its rusty filing cabinet and sorts through four different folders of operating info. There's one labeled Inglsh Langage, one labeled Large Motor Skills (which is just a disheveled mess), an empty one named Social Skills, and one labeled Involuntary Reflexes. My brain frantically flips through all of them but finds nothing relevant. It then sees a sticky note stuck to a pile of empty folders that reads "Just ask Siri." Useless. It'll be three days until we're in Alaska again where my iPhone can find friendly AT&T towers. Surely I can survive for three days relying on my instincts.

I can sum up the landscape we've been seeing for the last 24 hours: trains, grain bins, fields, trains, grain bins, fields. Then sometimes, in a shocking twist of events, we'd see trains, fields, grain bins. You'd notice they were in a different order! Interesting, huh? We drove through Alberta and Saskatchewan and noticed similar madness. You would think that with a name like Saskatchewan you would find Sasquatches, or something of similar interest but you'd be wrong. Add that to your brain files for when you're tempted to drive through Canada. Note: Boring.

I did find something interesting about Canada. Everyone insists on living in large, uncomfortable piles of humanity called "cities." In America we prefer to build suburbs around our city. That way you can have some warning before you just arrive, surprised, confused, and vulnerable into a city. You can tell you're getting closer to the city because you'll notice more gas stations, neighborhoods, and shopping malls growing in density. Then, predictably, you'll find yourself locking the car doors and trying to find your way out of the inner city while ducking behind your steering wheel to avoid gunfire.

You have no one to blame but yourself. In Canada they just skip the suburb nonsense and go straight from desolate prairie to honking gridlock in about a quarter mile. We were driving through flat nothingness for hours on

end when suddenly we happen upon a city called Edmonton which was full of traffic jams. We sat in a traffic jam for an hour, inching forward an inch at a time, bringing new meaning to the term inching forward. We ate lunch at a Mexican burrito place, used the Wifi and toilets while emitting immense sighs of relief, and headed north again.

Somewhere in Saskatchewan I discovered the gas cap is missing. Matt simply reached his hand into a dark corner inside the RV and pulled out an old plastic bag. He stuffed it into the gas tank hole to keep the dirt and crud out of the gas. It works pretty well! We patted ourselves on the back for being environmentally friendly and resourceful.

Next memorable stop was Dawson Creek, British Columbia. This is where the fun begins since Dawson Creek is Mile 0 of the Alaska Highway.

Note: Dawson Creek is right on the border of British Columbia and Alberta, but is located inside British Columbia. This is why it says "Alberta" on the building below.

We stopped at the sign commemorating the start of the Alaska Highway to take pictures and to marvel at the fact that Lame Duck RV was still running. We knocked on wood and started down the Alaska Highway. The terrain quickly begins to buckle, pine tree forests begin to thicken, and wildlife – including mosquitoes – begin to get bigger and more dangerous. It's the first in my life that I've seen the GPS show the next turn is in 950 miles.

By this time I'm a huge fan of Tim Hortons – so much so that I'm fairly twitching in my enthusiasm for their coffee. I've heard of Tim Hortons from my Canadian friends but assumed they were being a bit melodramatic since they had nothing else to get excited about in Canada. I was wrong; Tim Hortons is excellent!

British Columbia is amazing. The scenery is breathtaking, wild, and free. It feels like you have to sit in one place and just stare for days to absorb what's in front of you. We saw a black bear, a moose, and two bison so far. I've seen more exciting wildlife driving down the Alaska Highway for six hours than I did in a lifetime of hunting in Pennsylvania (Maybe that's just a reflection of my hunting skills). My only complaint with the jaw dropping scenery is that my mouth dries out from holding it open for so long. Not everyone is sold on the North's majesty. "Infatuation with the wild cold north has some of the people in this camper delusional," claims my wife, Janice. She's just cranky because she can't get on Facebook. Also, she has a rabid hatred for cold weather, something that the North has in spades.

UPDATE: Matt still didn't buy a fuel pump for the Lame Duck. It seems the old one is hanging in there so as long as it doesn't give out again, what's the point of buying a new one? Ha! It's good to avoid foolish excess in life.

Mile 422 of the Alaska Highway– Toad River Lodge! We often stop for gas here while on the way through.

We just got into the Yukon. The GPS now says 250 miles to the next turn, so that's progress! The plan to keep the wheels moving is working splendidly. Morale is mixed and seems to be based on the availability of coffee. The odor index is rapidly rising to intolerable levels thanks to the lack of bathing among the crew. I had washed my head with hand soap in a gas station's bathroom. It helped a little. I no longer notice the smell of the toilet in the back of the RV. Maybe it fixed itself. Maybe the waste tank just fell off of the bottom of the RV while we were airborne through that construction site. Maybe we all just burned off the sensory organs in our noses. Look out Alaska, we are getting closer!

Note from Matt: Josh took along stickers for his "Beard Balm" and proceeded to decorate nearly every sign we came across. On the sign above, his sticker graces the bottom of left side of the "U" in Yukon. Hopefully this type of thing is not illegal and he does not end up in jail over the mention in the book.

Just North of Normal: The Sign Post Forest, Yukon, Canada

Probably one of the most famous landmarks along the Alaska Highway is the Sign Post Forest located in Watson Lake, Yukon, Canada. The Sign Post Forest is exactly what it sounds like; a forest of signs. It's tradition is to bring a sign from your hometown and nail it up somewhere in the rings of posts all carrying dozens of signs of all sizes. New signs are added daily and in fact, there is over 77,000 unique signs hung in the forest. I even heard one being hammered in while I was visiting. Unfortunately I wasn't aware of this tradition before I left home, or I definitely would've purchased a road sign and threw it in the RV. Elkhart, Indiana was already represented, however, so my sign would have been a little redundant.

So who decided to start a Sign Post Forest anyway? Is this all they have to do in Canada? Are the sign companies trying to start a viral marketing scheme? Actually, the tradition dates back to the construction of the Alaska Highway in 1942. Carl Lindley was a homesick soldier helping construct the highway. In honor of his hometown, Carl hung a sign with his town's name on it on the mile marker at the corner of Watson Lake Airport Rd and the Alaska Highway where the Sign Post Forest still stands today.

Apparently homesick people like carrying around signs from their hometown and the tradition really caught on. Like most viral successes, Carl had no clue his idea would stick. He visited the area a few years later and was astonished at the amount of signs posted. There are now signs everywhere from everywhere, and it quickly become a time honored tradition, encouraged by the local authorities and maintained by the Rotary Club. There are signs from Germany, Switzerland, Colorado, Mexico, California, Florida, and every little town imaginable. It's really interesting to see all the international adventurers represented.

The real reason I think the forest is so popular is it's right at the point in your travels where you are on the brink of insanity from staring blankly at  pine trees and the hood ornament of your car for hours on end. It could be a collection of urinals and it would be a welcome distraction from the hours of driving you have left. So before you leave your hometown to travel the Alaska Highway, go buy a road sign! Keep the tradition alive!

The Lame Duck has made it to Alaska! I mean, we still have 19 hours of driving left so don't get too excited. In case you didn't know, Alaska is actually two and a half times the physical size of Texas. You don't realize that because on most maps Alaska is squashed and put in the lower left hand corner of the map. Understandably, the map makers aren't too concerned about offending people since Alaska has few in it. Case in point: 40% of Alaska residents live in one city; Anchorage. This means there are millions of acres of lonely, unspoiled wilderness chock full of bears, moose, caribou, wolverines, porcupines, elk, and all manner of animals just waiting to be found, shot, and eaten. Or, if you are a particular kind of stupid (like many tourists), there are millions of cute fuzzy animals waiting to be coddled.

Those Coca-Cola polar bears aren't quite as friendly as one might think. Anyway, here we are, rolling across the border into the promised land! The U.S. Border Patrol at the Alcan Border is really nice and understanding. "Hey folks, sorry you had to spend all that time in Canada." We profusely beg him to allow us in, and soon we were embracing the beautiful wilderness and freedom of Alaska.

Matt spots the Welcome to Alaska sign, which is about half a mile down the road from the border crossing, and guides the Lame Duck into the pull off so we can take pictures and prove that the Lame Duck actually made it the whole way. Afterwards I realized I never actually did take pictures of the RV beside the sign. It seemed to spoil the majesty of the sign.

I poke my sleeping wife – which is about as smart as waking a bear out of hibernation by slapping it repeatedly between the eyes – and point at the landscape. "Look! Alaska!"

She rubs her eyes. "Looks like Canada." She flops her head back onto her crossed hands while sighing wearily. It's understandable. Driving for five days in a rattling RV with 11 other people can make anyone delusional and pessimistic. Still, in retrospect, while her response was sort of disappointing I am lucky to still have my limbs intact.

We stumble out of the motor home bleary-eyed and grumpy. We snap a few pics and stumble back into the RV and tear off towards the horizon, leaving behind only swirling dust, a bumper, and a vent cover.

Driving has become much more interesting since the road is twisting, turning, climbing, and dropping like a roller coaster. You know those wood-en coasters that are really slow yet somehow so traumatic that they give you

Janice braided Josh's beard while he drove. I didn't even realize braided beards were the latest fashion. Below: Marlene and Missy comb the girls hair.

spinal fractures and near death experiences? That's the Alaska Highway. Among it's many standard, run-of-the-mill features such as potholes and hitchhikers in orange jumpsuits it also has small mountain ranges called "Frost Heaves" built into the road. They were built into the highway to keep drivers alert and on the verge of vomiting. Actually, it's Mother Nature's way of reminding mankind who is boss. When the ground freezes and thaws, it expands and contracts creating gigantic speed bumps in the road. Man can try to tame the wilderness but the wilderness usually gets in a few good punches before it submits.

The Alaska Highway is a feat of engineering, but the Mallard RV we're driving is not, and evidence of this is abundant. The fridge door swings open every fifth frost heave, causing bananas, lunch meat, Dr. Pepper, and Snapple Iced Tea to rattle around the RV interior, much like shaking a spray can. The suspension is compressing and exploding like a cheap accordion being played by a 500 pound gorilla. I'm holding on to the steering wheel like a sailor in a hurricane. Here's a quick tip for driving a cheap RV down the Alaska Highway; the best place to be is in the middle of the RV. This is because that's the pivot point – or the fulcrum – of the vessel and so your vertical height differences are minimal. Those are big words. Let me try to explain this in a scientific drawing:

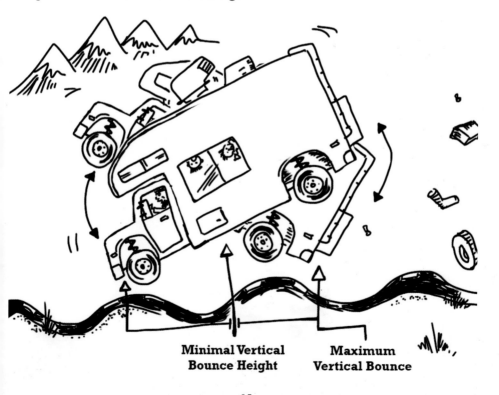

Minimal Vertical Bounce Height   **Maximum Vertical Bounce**

Then it started raining. That's not a big deal unless your windshield wipers didn't work. Did I mention that Lame Duck's windshield wipers didn't work? Driving down a highway with twists, turns, limited guard rails, and high drops while squinting through a river of water was intense to say the least. Thankfully Alaska is only dark for about two hours a night or so in the summer (it depends where you are at in Alaska) so that helped visibility immensely. Once it got dark, the driving was handed over to Matt. It was his idea to drive this piece of junk in the first place. Let him suffer.

My wife and I settled into a deep sleep together – which sounds romantic until you realize we were on the floor of the RV, right between the bananas and the lunch meat. It wasn't as bad as it sounds since the bananas and lunch meat softened the blows to our head. The rest of the trip is a blur since I was fading in and out of consciousness.

Things happened. We ate at some place called "Fast Eddies" in Tok, Alaska which sounds more like a used car mart than a pizza place but seriously, top notch joint. After that we had more driving and more misery. Some time later we arrive at my brother's "house" in Anchor Point, Alaska in the morning. We immediately stumble out of the RV, wipe the debris off ourselves, and find a solid surface to sleep on. We'll find adventure when we're not bone dog dead tired (is that a thing?). Stay tuned!

Fact Checking Josh's Blogs

So we arrive in Alaska, and Josh suddenly stops blogging. He may have been overcome with exhaustion, or perhaps, the fumes in the motorhome. Whatever the case, I'll take over again. But first: Some fact checking.

Myth #1: Matt's books read like they are proofread by a five-year-old foreign exchange student.

I'm fairly certain they don't let 5 year-old-children in the student exchange program. It is true there may be an occasional typo in our books. This may be a marketing ploy. It works like this: Jane Doe reads our book and is horrified to find the word *to* used instead of too. She quickly calls her friends, and says, "I can't believe this! There is a typo on this book on page so and so." Her friends, all used to reading books without any errors, are shocked. They quickly buy copies for themselves in order to see this error. Soon they are all calling their friends, and suddenly our book is a best seller, all because we were willing to sacrifice a little bit of grammar and/or spelling. Or, better yet: Perhaps a secret code is hidden in the seemingly random typos that lead to a fantastic buried treasure somewhere. I refuse to confirm or deny this...

Myth #2: Matt lives "part time" in Alaska.

This is true in the technical sense of the word. I don't die if I exit Alaska and suddenly revive upon return. However, last year (2015) the clear majority of the year we were in Alaska. This common mistake is made by people as described earlier in the book. It is also as absurd as saying someone lives in a portable toilet because you happened across them there. Sigh.

Myth #3: The air conditioner on the roof is making the carpet in the hallway wet.

The air conditioner on the roof did not work, therefore it is impossible that it made the floor wet. The leak was traced to a leaking pipe under the sink.

Myth #4: The fuel pump gave out but beating on the tank caused it to start working again.

This was not tested under laboratory conditions. Perhaps there is another explanation, such as the government was testing a top secret device to remotely shut off vehicles.

Myth #5: The wind in North Dakota would blow the motorhome in the air, causing only one tire to remain on the ground.

I'm fairly certain most of the tires were on the ground all the time. It is possible the phenomenon could be explained by the steering being loose, causing the driver to think the wheels were airborne.

Myth #6: Matt saved the day by forgetting to empty the sewage tank.

This depends on what Josh meant, the motor home has two sewage tanks. One for gray water (sink and shower water) and one for black water to which the toilet connects. The gray water tank emptied itself, due to a leak. So this would not have contributed any weight to the RV. Mysteriously, the black water tank never filled up either.

Myth #7: The motor home smelled like a well used portable toilet on a hot summer day.

I would say the smell was more comparable to an outhouse on a cool autumn day.

Myth #8: Matt invented a gas cap for the RV, using only a plastic bag.

This was actually the handiwork of a brilliant gas station attendant. I have used similar innovations in the past. Our theory is the gas cap may have been stolen by the same government agents testing the engine shutoff device.

Time to load up on energy!

Josh was right; I had secretly hoped Janice would fall head over heels in love with Alaska. After all, she fell for Josh. I figured once we had them both in Alaska, the weather would be beautiful, the birds in full song, and it would be a shoe in. Unfortunately, it seemed she developed AAD, or *Anti Alaska Disorder*. Alaska has this ability to detect when we have guests, and try to drive them away with bad weather. For example, last summer in July it was beautiful and clear, and it didn't rain for weeks, except, of course, when we had guests.

This year, we had the same deal. As soon as we arrived at our house, it started to rain. The weather was colder than normal, and it just wasn't ideal. When I informed Janice of this, she assumed I was stretching the truth and figured it was already warmer than normal. I think I may have ruined my reputation with her by dragging them 4,000 miles in the RV. To top it off, my 27' boat was in the shop getting fixed. It seems to spend most of its time in the shop getting fixed. The only way to go Halibut fishing was to book a charter, and Josh is a bit of a cheapskate.

My little 16' skiff also wouldn't start. The starter quit working, and there were no starters that fit the motor within 2,000 miles. I ordered a starter from the lower 48, but shipping is somewhat slow.

Naturally, the generator also quit working, and the backup generator decided to also quit. This was also harmful to my sales pitch, but I was grateful things were going smoother than normal. Then one evening Josh announced they were going to the ER. Janice had pain in her mouth, so badly that she couldn't stand it. Or, they may have just been tired of our place and were looking for a way to politely leave. After all, the hospital was connected to the grid and always had running water.

After their stint at the hospital, they rented a car and went on a mini road trip up to Valdez. That was basically the last we heard of them for awhile. When we met up with them later, it was painfully obvious that they were not moving to Alaska.

In the meantime, I had the Mallard to deal with. I put some ads up, and waited for the calls to pour in. I had priced it at $6,000, which was probably a bit optimistic considering how it had deteriorated on the trip. Although, I could brag we had just rolled in from a 4,400 mile road trip with hardly any mechanical issues. Of course, the only issue we had was the motorhome shutting off, which may have just been that secret government conspiracy. At first the calls were a trickle. Some guy called from Australia, of all places. He wanted to wire money, and it may have been a scam.

One day we hiked back to the Russian River Falls. You can see salmon jumping up the falls, and often there are bears here. But we didn't see any bears!

I didn't really want to bother with all that hassle anyway. Next, some lady wanted to meet me in Soldotna and look at it. However, she backed out before I could make it up there.

A fellow texted me and asked if I would consider trading the motorhome for a boat. After my previous experiences with boats, this got a chuckle out of me. After all, "boat" stands for "bail out another thousand (dollars!)" But, I decided to look over the boat this guy was trying to pawn off on me. He probably had experienced a string of setbacks and was at the end of his rope, so to speak. Even though I didn't want another boat (of course), it might really be an encouragement to him if I traded the motorhome for the boat. Maybe he needed a place to live and was camping underneath the boat. I would be doing him a real favor by trading the motorhome for his boat, and it would only be right to help him out.

A day or two later I met him in the Fred Meyers parking lot. At first I thought I had the wrong guy, as I had to admit the boat was nicer than I expected. My steel-like resolve to avoid boats for now and forever was beginning to show signs of degradation. I have found that living near large bodies of salt water does this to resolve avoiding boat purchases.

There was a huge hurdle to cross (aside from my extreme reluctance), before this transaction would even be considered. First, Bob, the potential boat trader, would need to inspect the motorhome. As I wheezed and clanked up beside him, I was worried this would throw him into fits of laughter. After all, he was advertising his boat and trailer for $8,000. The rotted out rattle trap I had paid $2,500 for, and I was beginning to doubt it was even worth that.

The boat was an 18 foot aluminum hull Lund. It had a 150 HP outboard, a brand new fish finder (that I later priced at $800) and a passel of other goodies. The trailer it was on was in very nice shape. It was even set up for saltwater fishing with a nice light bar over the boat, and with rod holders.

Bob did check the motorhome out, and even took pictures of it. "I'll have to see what my wife says," he told me. I figured Bob, being very polite, didn't want to laugh his tonsils out in front of me. He would disappear, and I would likely never hear from him again. I agreed that it was only reasonable he show his wife (if he actually had one), and we parted ways, but not before he pointed out that the Mallard was leaking gasoline all over the parking lot. This was easily fixed with a bit of rubber fuel line, but backed up my theory that Bob would "fly the coop."

What would your choice be? A boat-or a Mallard?

I called up my buddy Marv and asked him what he thought of trading the motorhome for the boat. His advice was to drop everything I did, and do it immediately. Later I talked to Marlin Eicher, and he called me a "thief." Hmm, it was sounding like maybe the boat was worth more than the motorhome. Then, to my astonishment, Marlene even gave a nod of approval. It wasn't so much that she was infatuated with the boat, but that she was more worried the motorhome would fall apart before we could find a buyer. If Marlene approves something, it's almost a guaranteed winner.

Later in the week, Bob called again. He wanted to meet at the airport, where he worked. Turns out he was in charge of the fuel desk, refueling jets and so forth. So I took the Mallard over to the airport, and he went over it again. Naturally, the generator decided to quit working. It had worked our entire trip, up until this day.

Bob took the motorhome for a short drive and commented how nice it drove. It actually does drive fine, if not being buffeted by high winds on the prairie. Aware of Marlin's perspective that the motorhome was worth (far) less than the boat, I tried to point out every problem with the RV (so as to avoid the title of "con artist"). This took awhile. Nothing seemed to phase Bob. Even when I pointed out the roof had soft spots, he just laughed. When I pointed out the leak in the graywater tank valve, he chuckled. "All motorhomes' sewer valves leak," he said. I didn't want to get in an argument, but I was pretty sure I didn't see other motorhomes leaving a trail of sewage in their wake.

After I pointed out the leaking pipe under the sink, he scoffed. "I'm planning to rip out the sink and replace it," he said. It turned out he was planning to gut the whole interior and redo it. Bob was a do-it-yourself type, and wanted a project. This was a project all right.

After talking about all the motorhome's issues, I was about ready to give it away for free. Then Bob's negotiation skills came out. He suggested that his boat may be worth more than the motorhome. This was a difficult point to refute. My mouth felt a bit dry. What if Bob walked off, and I was stuck trying to sell this heap of junk to someone else, who didn't want a project? I offered him the motorhome plus $1,250 in cash for his boat. He seemed delighted with this offer, and we exchanged titles. Despite the fact I had another money hungry boat to deal with, I actually felt pretty elated.

This boat acquisition led to another issue: Boating itself. I asked Marlene to go boating with me, and she refused, saying she didn't feel like boating. Furthermore, she stated I wasn't to go boating and let her sit at home by herself, but I was to wait for her. Oh, the agony! It seemed like I was

73

stuck outside of time and space; glaciers rose, then melted. Nations came and went, saplings turned into Giant Sequoias, died of old age, and rotted to the ground. Finally, a full day later, Marlene said she was ready to go out in the boat. Missy came down to watch the younger children while we went boating (she was staying with Calvin Yoder's).

The 150 hp Mercury roared to life. This was a pleasant surprise, as not all my past boats were so workable. The *Sergeant* would take about a can of starting fluid before it would fire up. The *Lund* also had a small "kicker" motor, in case the big engine would fail out on the water. It was hard to imagine having such luxury on a boat. We also decided to name the new boat the *Mallard*.

We cruised around Cook Inlet on the *Mallard*. It was great to use a more capable boat. The little 16' skiff was great, but it wouldn't go more than 15 mph. The skiff also had lower sides, and would take on water quicker. The *Lund* was designed to handle 6 foot seas without a problem. It had a top speed of 45 mph, which was much faster than I really wanted to go. On water everything seems faster than on land.

The weather was rainy, but we still stayed out a few hours. Previously I had described a time warp phenomenon to Marlene regarding boats, but it was obvious she hadn't believed me. The phenomenon is this: Time goes slower (or faster depending on your perspective) on a boat. You are out boating for 25 minutes, while on shore (or in the cabin), an hour or two has gone past. The result is you're out in the boat 45 minutes, but to people who are not boating, you have been out 3 or 4 hours. Marlene realized this was actually factual, although it has not been proved in laboratory conditions. This is mostly because it is difficult to fit a lake and boat inside a laboratory.

In the brief time we were out on the water we tried our hand at fishing. Unfortunately we caught no fish. Before hardly any time passed, it was time to return to the dock. We had agreed to meet Missie at the dock at a predetermined time. To maximize time in the water, she had actually dropped us off. I was surprised Missie had been able to turn the van and trailer around at our place (she had returned to our place after dropping us off).

This was actually the first time I had Marlene with me in my own boat. Last year she had gone along on a charter, but that doesn't really count. This fact may explain her sometimes hostile attitude towards boats. I resolved to do better in the future and take her out more often!

Above: The most magnificent boat I have owned, the all aluminum hull 18 foot *Lund*, with 150 HP outboard. Below: The small boat harbor at Homer, Alaska. My favorite harbor-in the whole world!

Amish in Alaska!
Chapter 13

People often ask me (and I'm not quite sure why) if there are Amish in Alaska. Yes! There are Amish in Alaska, at least there were this past summer at my place. I have it on good authority there are more coming. But let me explain. We have friends who are Amish, and love to travel as much as we do. Their names are Henry and Nancy Swarey, and they have three children, Samuel age 12, Moses age 9, and Andrew age 6. Amish don't fly, but they do ride trains, boats and automobiles. Henry and Nancy live in Mifflintown, Pennsylvania.

I don't remember their complete trip itinerary, but basically they took the train from Pennsylvania to Seattle, Washington. From there they took another train north into Canada. There they encountered a high strung customs lady that declared, "Today you are not getting into Canada!". This was because they did not have a photo ID. However, you can cross into Canada without photo ID, so this situation was straightened out after finding a manager. This delay almost had them miss their next train, but they managed to catch it. From Vancouver, they caught a boat north to Seward, Alaska.

We picked up the Swarey's with our white 15 passenger van, pulling Alan Reinford's trailer for luggage. Because Seward was already on the way to the interior, we had decided to pick them up and head up to the Arctic Circle. After checking that out, we were going to head over past Fairbanks and try panning for more gold.

Our original plan was to pick Henry's family up in the motorhome, then head north. Last year we had taken the motorhome on the "Haul Road," also known as the Dalton Highway, and it didn't take it really well. A few days prior to the Swarey's arrival I had some issues with the motorhome's electrical system. Nothing major, but significant enough I didn't want to just drive it off into the wild blue yonder. The biggest issue was actually procrastination on my part. After some thought, it seemed like it might be just less hassle to drive the van and trailer and get motels. The van gets 14 mpg; the motorhome gets 6 or 7, depending which way the wind is blowing. With the van we could also make better time, especially on rough roads.

It is about a 9 hour drive to Fairbanks from Seward. The trip went smoothly, and we found a motel in Fairbanks with rooms. A group our size took three rooms, as we had Missy along for the trip. We took advantage of her room by stuffing some extra children in with her. Hopefully she didn't mind.

Above: The route to Anchorage. Below: This lake is totally breathtaking.

The next day we hit the road around 8 am. It's a fairly long day, driving to the Arctic circle and back to Fairbanks, but it can be done. We didn't want to push it hard either, as everyone wanted to see the scenery. Don't try to draw a map with this information, but I think we came to the Haul Road about an hour and a half drive outside of Fairbanks. From there it was another several hours to the Arctic circle.

Our first bit of drama came because of a small oversight on my part. My imagination can be very creative. In this instance, it imagined plentiful amounts of gas stations along the Haul Road. I'm not sure why my mind was playing such tricks on me. As we neared the Haul Road, we passed a gas station. I should have topped off the tank, but it was showing above 3/4 tank. Naturally, I had neglected to throw our two spare gas cans in the trailer. I did have about a half gallon of gas for the water pump, which was to be used later on the trip, for gold panning. A tip for travel in the north: Carry lots of gas with you. You will never regret having extra gas along. The same goes for water, but water is easier to find than gas. In a pinch you can drink water out of a creek.

As we merely drove along, I watched the 3/4 full gauge slowly drop. "Just around the next bend I think there is a nice gas station," I found myself saying frequently. As we rolled on and on, I started to wonder what would happen if we did run too low on gas to get back to the last gas station we passed, right before the Haul Road started. It wouldn't have been nice to stop short of the Arctic Circle sign, and tell everyone "too bad, we are heading back." I knew there was a gas station in Coldfoot, which would be about a two hour drive past the Arctic circle sign. This demonstrates how remote the Arctic Circle is, as we were looking at two hours to Coldfoot, vs four hours back to the closest gas station we passed. That would mean getting to Fairbanks very late.

It was time for lunch, so we stopped along a pull off beside the road. We simply started a fire on the gravel and grilled some hot dogs and sausages. Henry likes Sunny Delight, and had a few gallons of it along. I hate Sunny Delight. It stems back to when I was in first grade. The school (Gehman's Mennonite School) either ran out of real orange juice, or replaced it with some wanna be orange drink. Being young and naive, I got the fake orange drink, not knowing it wasn't orange juice. This putrid substance I nearly spit all over my desk. I'm still upset about it, and have hated fake orange juice ever since. But enough boring flashbacks.

We had plenty of water, and also some soft drinks along. However, Henry also sells healthy energy drinks. I really like the way they taste, but

Above: We made a campfire and roasted some hotdogs. Below: An illustration of roasting the hotdogs over the fire. Next time I'll make a thinner version of myself.

Above: Our van and Alan's trailer. Below: I should have had some of Josh's beard stickers along. Looks like other people had the same idea.

I'm a bit of a cheapskate, except when it comes to purchasing real orange juice. All I needed to do was yawn and swerve off the road, and Henry would hurriedly offer me a free energy drink. I got lots of free energy drinks this way.

While eating lunch, we discussed our fuel dilemma. It was decided to drop the small enclosed trailer at the pullout, and continue on without the trailer. On the way back we would pick it up, unless someone had stolen it. In that case, I would have to go shopping for a replacement trailer for Alan. The mosquitoes seemed to get worse the further north we got. I must admit mosquito spray doesn't seem all that healthy for a person, but hanging out in swarms of mosquitoes quickly reduces your aversion to it.

After our lunch we continued on our way, without the trailer. You run across all types of people on the Dalton Highway, as it is the road to Prudhoe Bay. This is the furthermost point north you can drive in the United States, and so it is a popular starting point or destination for people. You want to bike across North America? Might as well start at Prudhoe Bay. Want to take a trip on a unicycle? It works for that too. I actually saw a guy driving what might be described as a "cross country unicycle." I didn't talk to him, so maybe he was just heading to town for groceries. So it was no surprise we came across an antique car. Before long we passed it and continued on our way. Just for the record, I don't have any problem with people starting long trips or finishing them at Prudhoe Bay. I think it's a great idea! The only downside is that all the cool ideas are taken already.

Soon we came to a place called "Finger Rock." We stopped to check it out, and the children released their energy by bouncing all over the rocks. One favorite past time of our children is injuring themselves. They just are not happy if they are not getting hurt. Henry's children proved to be the same way. Samuel quickly ran over to a rock and twisted his ankle. Shane wasted no time trying to copy the stunt, except I ordered him off the rocks before he could manage it. He sighed, as if not being allowed to injure yourself was a form of torture.

While we were trying to keep the children from further injuries, the guy driving the old car pulled in. Naturally, we wanted to know what he was doing and where he was from. His name was Bob, and he was from Illinois. His car was a 1931 Model A Ford, and he drove it the whole way from Illinois. He reported having some trouble with the water pump in Montana, but otherwise was running great. The car got 17 mpg. At some point in the future Bob plans to drive the Model A to Key West, Florida. I didn't tell Bob, but Key West is actually a pretty boring place.

Above: The children playing on rock formations near "Finger Rock." Below: The actual Finger Rock, located a distance away from the other rocks.

Bill and the Model A Ford. The screen was to protect the classic car from the many rocks and debris encountered on the Dalton Highway.

$ [   ] THIS SALE

4.123
GALLONS
PRICE/GALLON

$ [   ]
TAXES INCLUDED

NLEADED

After about half an hour to stretch our legs at Finger Rock, we continued north. The fuel gauge was still dropping with no gas stations in sight. We were almost at half a tank, which was the point of no return. We crossed the Yukon River, and noticed a building and some vehicles up ahead on the left. It didn't look hopeful, but we decided to stop in anyway. Sure enough, they had gas! It was low octane, and a salty $5.49 a gallon. But expensive gas is still cheaper than a cheap tow truck (and there are no cheap tow trucks in Alaska)!

I was glad to be able to fill the tank. It does annoy me when gas station charges a lot more, just because they are in the middle of nowhere. But I believe in the free market. They didn't force me to come and buy gas, and I could always start a gas station across the street and undercut them. But it's not worth the effort for me to do that, and apparently it's not worth that effort for anyone else.

After bumming another energy drink from Henry, I finished filling the tank, and we headed north. About this time we caught up to some pickup trucks pulling campers. If you value your camper any bit, you will take your time on the Dalton Highway. Not having the trailer hooked up, I passed them without any trouble.

Allow me to go down a bunny trail a little bit. I say this with all attempts at modesty and do not mean to brag. When I first started writing, I never really gave the repercussions much thought. But if you start writing books about your life and load them with pictures, then sell thousands of books, complete strangers start to recognize you. Sure, I expected people to recognize the limo, but I never thought they would start recognizing me.

Since we have been selling books, I have had people run up to me while stopped at traffic lights, in the store, auctions, and all sorts of random places. Except for the guy that cornered me in a grocery store, demanding to know my ancestry, it has all been very positive. I certainly don't mind people saying hi, commenting on the books, etc. All that to say, on the drive to the Arctic Circle, I specifically remember thinking (with a subconscious chuckle) "Nobody at the Arctic Circle sign will recognize me."

It had been three years and one month since our first (and only) visit to the Arctic Circle sign. The sign looked pretty much exactly as it had three years ago. We milled around the sign for a little bit, I snapped some pictures, then we prepared to load everyone in the van. About that time the one truck towing the camper pulled in. The driver got out of the truck and walked up to us. "So are you the author?" he asked. I was dumbfounded. I replied that I did write some books, and sure enough, he had read several of my books. He

Above: Ervin and Alma Miller at the Arctic Circle sign parking lot. They are from Arkansas. Below: An illustration of our families in front of the Arctic Circle sign.

said they recognized me when we passed them.

The couple's names were Ervin and Alma Miller. They were from Arkansas. They were traveling with his brother Sylvan and his wife, who were driving the other truck and camper. I asked them if they knew Lloyd Troyer, who lived in Sterling. Lloyd and Esther were also from Arkansas. He replied they did, and that they were actually going to be staying at their place. I think he may have also been related to Lloyd, but my memory is failing me on that point. They were planning to camp overnight at the Arctic Circle sign, and I think they were considering going the whole way to Prudhoe Bay. However, I am not 100% sure of this.

I should say this about the Arctic Circle sign, it's almost as boring as Key West, Florida. But being able to casually drop the fact you were there into social conversations makes it worth it (Alaska too, for that matter). For example, in high school I was a really boring person. My clothes were bland, my car ugly (my dad's van, which I drove half the time because my car was broken down, was even uglier), I was pretty much broke, and I didn't get very good grades.

Fast forward 15 years. I go to a high school reunion, and everyone is sitting around being polite making small talk. I'm still driving an ugly car, still almost broke, and have bland clothes. But drop the fact you spent the last two years living in a shack in Alaska, carrying a big rifle and chasing the wolves out of your chicken pens, and suddenly you're the life of the party. If that isn't good enough, you just show off some pictures of a 50 pound Halibut you caught. All that to point out, if you're not cool, just go to Alaska and you suddenly become a cool person (in more ways than just one).

On the way back we stopped in and picked up the trailer. As we came up to the spot where the trailer was parked, we joked about the guys in the vehicle ahead of us trying to steal it. To our surprise, they pulled in ahead of us where the trailer was parked, and quickly left again when we showed up. It was probably just a coincidence, but everyone loves a good conspiracy.

We arrived back in Fairbanks around 9 P.M. feeling famished. Everyone agreed they were hungry for Chinese food, but we figured that would probably be an almost impossible find. To our shock and delight, we found a Chinese restaurant that was open! We quickly ran in, except for Samuel, who was hopping because his ankle was still sprained. Here it became obvious that Moses (Henry's son), likes ketchup. He drank it straight from the ketchup bottle! That is until Henry put a stop to it (I should also include some of my children's bad habits-but I'm so used to them I can't remember any). After a very good meal, it was off to the motel again. The next day our plan was to visit the same spot we had panned for gold last year.

Around 8 A.M. we rolled out of the motel, this time going on the Steese Highway, towards Circle. It is 161 miles from Fairbanks to Circle, but we didn't plan on going the whole way to Circle. After a few false alarms, we found the right pull off. It looked the same as it did a year ago when we were here, but this time we had extra hands to carry the equipment. With Henry and his boys helping, we hauled the gold panning equipment down the ravine in one trip. Henry carried the shotgun, affectionately named "Mabel", and I carried my .454 revolver. Unfortunately no bears bothered us.

Henry is highly motivated, and never does anything half halfhearted-ly. With the water pump set up and running, we all set to shoveling dirt into the sluice. If there was any gold in that creek, we would find it! Sadly, we found no gold. I secretly began to doubt my gold prospecting skills. Missy was along, and she seemed to be of the opinion that prospecting for gold was a form of insanity. Thankfully, nobody else seemed to share her thoughts. She seemed to be in a wild rush to get back to Sterling.

After shoveling, cleaning the sluice, and more shoveling, we found a few specks that looked interesting. I put them in a small vial for later obser-vations, which revealed it was not gold. Later, in Nome, we found real gold. After you handle the real thing, it is very easy to tell the difference!

Our gold panning spot

The mountain stream is very nice, but not a good place for gold prospecting. But, the thing about gold is that it could be right around the next bend. As I mentioned in an earlier book, gold prospecting is basically a socially approved form of gambling.

Hauling all the equipment back up the ravine was a chore, but with all the hands it went quickly. It was a let down not finding any obvious gold nuggets, but I can't say anyone was too surprised. Returning to Fairbanks, we encountered a small problem: There were no motels available. Well, that wasn't quite true, we did find some for about $379 a room near Denali National Park. In our minds, that was the same as not finding any. Henry told the motel, "we are not rich people", so they gave us a number for another motel. Those rooms turned out to be "only" $279 each! We kept trying to find motel rooms further south, and finally found some in Wasilla for a reasonable price. The only problem: Wasilla was an 8 hour drive away! It was around 4 P.M., which meant we would arrive around midnight. This was assuming, of course, that we didn't stop to take pictures or for bathroom breaks.

We drove through some rain on the way back through Denali, and encountered several fantastic rainbows. This one is a double rainbow. It was one of the brightest rainbows I have ever seen. At first the rainbow showed up as just a light band, but it grew brighter and more distinct as we drove.

After stopping several times to take pictures, we decided these last photos were the best. Unfortunately, pictures just don't do justice to how it looked in real life. We thought maybe we should try panning for gold at the end of the rainbow, as it couldn't be worse than our other spot.

Some more pictures from the area around Denali. I have heard that the best time to take photos is around sunset or sunrise. It would seem that is correct.

As we drove south towards Wasilla, I got a call from Gareth Byers. After some polite small talk, he asked where I was. "Bummer," he said. "I was hoping you could go rescue Ben." This got me curious. What kind of situation was going on that I could possible be a rescuer in? "Ben's out on Cook Inlet, and his boat is sinking," Gareth said, rather non-nonchalantly. Before you jump to the conclusion that Gareth is hardhearted, remember he has been in Alaska for quite a few years. After awhile, these things kind of wear off on you.

This was also summertime, which meant the inlet was full of boats. The worst problem for Ben would have been needing to swim in the water for a few minutes, until another boat came over and picked him up. In all reality, for a typical boat owner, having your boat sink is a bit of a relief. This is especially the case if you have insurance. Who wouldn't want to send their troubles to the bottom of Cook Inlet?

Because we weren't home, we were not able to be of any assistance to Ben. Our place in Anchor Point is closer to Homer than anyone else at church, which would have put me in a position to respond quickest, in theory. In real life, probably most people from church could beat me to Homer. Thankfully some boats, already on the inlet, responded to the distress call on the radio, which was put out by the Coast Guard. Ben's boat was rescued, but just barely.

At midnight Shane turned 12 (July 13) so we all sang "Happy Birthday" to him! Now he insists on being called a "tween." In Alaska drivers can get their permit at 14. I used to think that was a great idea, now I'm not nearly as sure!

We did reach our motel in Wasilla, but not until about 2:30 A.M. This called for some sleeping in the next day. That evening we made it to our place in Anchor Point. We probably wouldn't have pushed as hard, but for some strange reason Missie wanted to get back really bad to Sterling.

The Shaw Family's Bus & Boat

96

I first met Ben and Jeanette Shaw in 2015 at the Sterling Mennonite Church summer picnic, right before we headed north on our (failed) gold prospecting trip. They were up to check out the area and see if they wanted to move there. They have thirteen children, which were not along at the time. Later I heard they were planning to indeed move to Alaska from New York. Anyone who moves to Alaska with thirteen children has my respect and admiration.

Fast forward to July, 2016. The Shaws had moved to Alaska, and brought the entire family along, except for an older child or two that had gotten married. I did not know the Shaws well, but was familiar with them when Gareth called, informing me of their sinking boat problem.

Later, I talked to Ben to ask him how this boat drama worked out, figuring it would be interesting material to write about. This speculation proved correct, and I am pleased to bring you the story of Ben's boat. The story actually starts with a sealed bid school district bus auction. Someone alerted Ben about this auction, because with 13 children you can always use a bigger vehicle. Ben gave a sealed bid of $1,500 and ended up winning the auction for a school bus with 106,000 miles on it. This vehicle was added to the family fleet. Hearing about this also gave me a few ideas for future purchases, but that's a later story.

At some point in time I believe the Shaws replaced the school bus with a newer one, the one they actually drove to Alaska. Initially they planned to pull their old mini van up behind the school bus, but suddenly happened on the realization that old mini vans are also cheap and in good supply in Alaska. What was not cheap and in good supply was big boats. Using this logic, they decided to scrap the mini van idea and just buy a big boat to pull behind the bus. This is quite admirable, although I used similar logic with almost disastrous results.

Ben found a nice boat for sale in New Jersey. The boat was a fiberglass 1998 27' Bayliner Trophy. One day Ben and one of his sons headed down to take it for a test drive. The boat performed flawlessly, and they went ahead with the purchase. The seller even threw in a free boat trailer with the deal. I have learned from experience that "free" boat trailers are not to be trusted, and this life lesson was soon to be also imparted on Ben.

After loading up the boat, they headed back to New York. As they cruised along, Ben noticed the boat was listing slightly to the side. Figuring he was dealing with a flat tire, he pulled over to check it out. All the tires looked good, so Ben decided the boat must have just been loaded crooked. He pulled out on the highway and continued on his way.

Glancing in the mirror, Ben thought the boat looked even more crooked than before. As he watched, the boat suddenly listed some more. Now he knew there was a problem! Quickly taking the next exit, Ben pulled over in a motel parking lot, only to be chased out by the owner. In a race against time, he found another motel. He explained to the front desk that he was having a problem with his boat trailer, and asked if he could rent a room and work on the trailer in the parking lot. To his relief, permission was granted.

It was already late in the day, and the boat was now safely parked, so Ben just went to bed. In the morning he got up only to discover overnight the trailer had completely collapsed and the cross members were on the ground. It was now the weekend, which meant the trailer shops were closed. Ben called around anyway, and managed to locate the owner of a trailer shop at home. The fellow nicely came out anyway and sold Ben a new trailer, but this didn't completely solve the problem. Loading and unloading boats is very different than say, four wheelers. You can't just nicely back the boat off the trailer and pull up on the new one without water. The old trailer couldn't be moved, as it had fallen apart. It is hard to appreciate this problem unless you yourself have tried to move boats around without water (folks may be shocked to learn I have experience with this).

Ben solved the dilemma by purchasing several jacks and jack stands. He blocked and jacked, blocked and jacked, until he had the boat raised off the old trailer. He then cut the old trailer apart and pulled it out from underneath the boat. The new trailer was carefully backed underneath the nose of the boat, and slowly winched on. This is a delicate situation, as boats like this are very heavy. If they fall halfway on or off the trailer they can be easily damaged. Finally, the boat was safely nestled on the trailer, and they continued home to New York. It was then transported to Alaska behind the bus. Ben can be thankful that the boat trailer didn't decide to hold together until the Alcan. I suspect boat trailers are a lot more expensive and not nearly as readily available along the Alaskan Highway as they are along the coast of New Jersey.

The Shaw family drove to Alaska and settled in without incident, or at least with no boat or boat trailer problems. They took the boat out on Cook Inlet several times, with no problems at all. Unlike the trailer, the boat decided to lure them into a false sense of security before causing problems.

Above: The Shaw children with Jeanette's father, with the new boat behind them.
Below: The boat blocked up with the new trailer sitting beside it.

After several trips, they took the boat out with some visitors from Ohio. This was in July, the exact same day we were driving back from Fairbanks with the Swarey family. Ben had his son Andrew along, and the five people from Ohio. After fishing near Tutka Cove (just below Seldovia where we fished with Henry) they decided to head out to Flat Island. This island is roughly 30 miles from the dock in Homer. They were cruising along, when suddenly the boat started running roughly. Ben shut the boat off and popped up the engine cover. The Bayliner had an inboard 250 HP 350 Mercruiser V-8 (basically a small block Chevy engine, but built to marine specifications). Under the engine was some water, but not much. It is normal for boats to have a small amount of water in the bilge, so Ben was not alarmed. He started the engine and went a bit further but was not able to go fast. They decided to just go fishing where they were, and Ben got out the fishing rods and tackle.

As they were pleasantly fishing, Ben noticed water coming up out of the deck drains. The drains are supposed to take water away, not spit water out. This seemed peculiar. Then Ben noticed the swim deck on the back of the boat was under water. Quickly he pulled the engine cover off again. To his horror, the engine was nearly covered in water!

Ben tried to start the boat, because in a boat, if you move forward through the water it will automatically lift the boat up. But the engine wouldn't start! Imagine sitting 20-30 miles from the dock, in a sinking boat, and not quite sure what to do. As Ben said, "I am just a farmer from upstate New York" and not accustomed to dealing with marine emergencies. Nothing wrong with farming or farmers; had the boat been a baler he could have probably wired it right back together. The people that were along on the boat were equally unfamiliar with boats.

Ben told everyone, "Ok guys, we got a serious problem here," and then, "Put your life jackets on, that water is on the wrong side of the fiberglass." I personally thought that was some quick wit for the situation, considering I probably would have run around while yelling loudly. Ben also put a call in to the Coast Guard, informing them of their problem. The Coast Guard put out an alert over the marine radio, and a nearby boat responded to help. Ben also called Gareth, who then called me. The problem is even had I been home in Anchor Point, by the time I drove to Homer, launched my boat, and proceeded 25 miles to Ben, it would have been at least 2 hours later. By that time the only thing left of the problem would have been bubbles in the water.

The boat that first responded had a hand-operated water pump, which they immediately put to use. This pump helped slow the sinking of the boat but could not pump the water out faster than it came in. Another vessel came on the scene that had been out fishing for several days and was returning to Homer. The captain of this boat, which was called "Fiat Lux" (Latin for "Let There be Light") was a boat mechanic and very familiar with marine situations. He immediately took over, jumped into the stricken boat, and fired up their very large, powered water pump. In a few minutes the bilge was emptied of water and the swim deck was where it was supposed to be.

The water was getting in from a previous repair that was not performed correctly. Above the outdrive in the back of the boat there was a little cover that was supposed to be bolted on. Someone had taken it off, and put it back on with only caulk, and no bolts. This eventually came loose, and started letting water in, climaxing with the excitement of the seal failing completely and letting water pour in like a broken fire hydrant.

After the leak was fixed, the *Fiat Lux* graciously offered to tow Ben's boat back to the dock, since it no longer started. The trip back took four hours, because you can't go very fast towing. After reaching the dock, the tow boat graciously refused to accept even a dime for payment. Ben took his boat to the same place I take my boat for repairs. They told him he was fortunate, as he didn't get any water in the engine, so it only took minor repairs ($6,000 worth) to get it working again. Did I mention I'm thinking about becoming a boat mechanic?

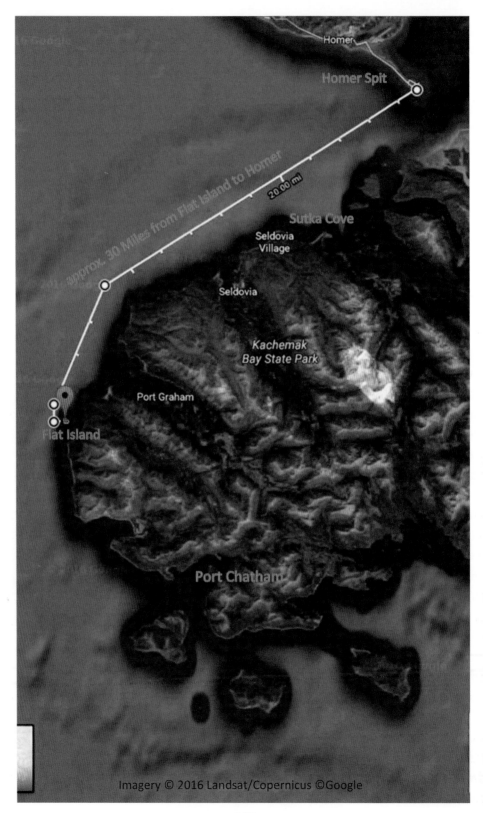

Homer

Homer Spit

20.00 mi

approx. 30 Miles from Flat Island to Homer

Sutka Cove

Seldovia
Village

Seldovia

Kachemak
Bay State Park

Port Graham

Flat Island

Port Chatham

Imagery © 2016 Landsat/Copernicus ©Google

Fishing with Henry
Chapter 15

Henry did not realize how close the fishing came to never happening. He can thank the Mallard (the motorhome, not the boat) for the fishing we did when his family visited. As stated earlier, my little skiff motor had developed a bad starter. I did order a replacement, but shipping to Alaska takes awhile. The large 27 foot boat was busy in the marine shop burning through $100 bills at a fast clip and not able to take us out.

Previous to the Mallard's entry into our life, I was contemplating our fishing options for the Swarey family's visit. We could fish from the beach, which is barely better than not fishing. My neighbor, Richard, enjoyed fishing from the river banks. But halibut do not come up the rivers, so we would never catch any halibut that way. As it worked out, the new boat showed up just in the nick of time. Unfortunately, Josh and Janice left literally a day or two before I took possession of it, so they were unable to go fishing. The way their trip had been going, it's probably good they didn't go out in the boat, or it might have sunk.

I had some other options for boats, none of them good. Gareth had generously offered to loan me his boat, if I repaired it. The issue was, the engine needed to be replaced. A perpetual need for repairs is a common theme with boats. That left Marlin and Alan. I decided not to even bother Alan, as he is always very generous. He would have probably loaned me his boat, but I was worried I would break it. Not only that, in the past year he had loaned me all kinds of things, including his truck. There was a high risk of crossing a line and being identified as a "moocher." Marlin doesn't even own his own boat, so I gave up on that thought before it started. Speaking of Marlin…

There are few people in this world who are smarter than Marlin. Don't give me jazz about college degrees and other rot. I know I have spoken of this in earlier books, but it is worth repeating. Marlin not only has a very nice aluminum boat to use, fit for Cook Inlet and the local rivers, he has not paid a dime for it. Not only did he not pay for the boat, he has a special checkbook just for the boat. If the boat needs a repair (as they often do) he just writes a check out of the magic checkbook, and someone else replenishes the checkbook balance. Sure, he has to put up with the actual owners showing up once a year and using the boat for a week or two, but that is a fairly minor inconvenience. And Marlin owns a house in Alaska, and Florida! Talk about having things figured out! But I digress. (My boat situation is exactly backwards, I just pay money out and never use the boat because something else breaks before it gets to the water.)

Anyway, complaining about boat problems won't get you on the water. It does solve the issue of people wanting to borrow my boats. Thankfully, the motorhome left the picture and was replaced with the 18' Lund described earlier in the book, which allowed us to plan our fishing trips on Cook Inlet.

After we returned to our place from our trip up north, it was time to go fishing. Because halibut rods cost $200 or more, I only had two of them. The limit for halibut is two fish a day, so we figured we would just take turns fishing. For halibut we use circle hooks, which are about 2 inches in diameter. One or two hooks can be used, baited with herring. The whole works is held down with two or four pound weights, depending on the tide current. Slack tide (the time between tides when water is the calmest) is usually the best time to fish.

Thursday morning we set out to Homer for our first try at halibut fishing. The weather was great. If you are planning a trip, one thing about fishing is, the weather can be fickle. You should plan your fishing expedition early in your Alaska trip, so you can reschedule it if necessary. Or better yet, just plan two or three trips, and one should work out. If they all work out, even better! Because of this, we planned to go fishing Thursday, Friday, and Saturday.

I wanted to make a good impression on Henry. Taking someone fishing is usually the worst way for me to impress people, although we did manage to hit it right last year when Conrad Brubaker's were visiting. Gareth told me fishing off the coast of Seldovia is almost a shoe in for catching halibut. Seldovia is a small town located towards the southern tip of the peninsula, accessible by boat or plane only. It is a little bit like Nome; no roads connect to the main road system. Past Seldovia is Port Graham, and then further south is Port Chatham.

Port Chatham is the abandoned town allegedly overrun with killer Bigfoots, also known as Sasquatches. There is also a scientifically questionable claim that it is also haunted by ghosts. Crazier still, supposedly the ghosts and Sasquatches co-conspire to scare people. Even more interesting, the Bigfoots and ghosts were the reason the townspeople all left, according to historical records. A place like that is too good not to check out! However, the object of the trip was fishing, not catching a Sasquatch. Besides, Port Chatham was about a 40 mile boat ride. I did not feel like taking my untested boat a two hour one way ride from the dock. Seldovia is about 15 miles, which is far enough.

Above: Fishing in the Lund

Below: The coast of Seldovia

The first day of fishing couldn't have gone better. We had six people on the boat, Henry and his three boys, Samuel, Moses, and Andrew. Then there was myself and Shane. That gave us a limit of 12 halibut. We launched out of Homer. After heading down to Seldovia, we found a group of boats and dropped anchor. It didn't take long for the fish to start biting!

It took an hour or two to catch our 12 halibut. In addition to the halibut, we caught three sharks and a salmon. I don't remember who caught what. I think Henry, Moses and Andrew caught the sharks, and Shane caught the salmon. The sharks were spiny dogfish sharks, ugly looking little things about 30 inches long.

The sun was shining, the sea calm. It was the best day of fishing I had ever had in my life. The boat worked flawlessly; the fish were biting. It just could hardly get any better. After we limited out, we headed back. The only problem with catching 16 large fish is that you have to filet and pack 16 large fish! But it is a great problem to have, one I'll take any day over not catching fish. With Henry, his boys, Shane, and myself all tackling the fish, it didn't take long to process. I think we might have caught a cod and some other fish too, but I don't bother counting them.

While the others were fishing I took the drone out and took it for a quick flight. I was a little nervous, as obviously if it falls out of the sky and hits the water, that is the end of it. However, on the water there are no trees to hit. The flight went without any wrecks, but Henry did catch a fish right in the middle of the flight, and I had to let the drone hover while we hauled the fish in. The drone can fly for 20+ minutes on a battery charge, so it wasn't a problem.

Butchering the sharks was a new experience. Sharks don't have a skeleton. They basically have a large strip of cartilage running down their back, surrounded by guts and meat. You can't filet them. What we did is just chop them up and separate the meat from everything else. Shark skin is coarse like sand paper. They were very easy to handle, unlike wet, slippery salmon and halibut. None of us had ever tried fresh shark, so we immediately fried one up in a pan. Marlene protested at first, being afraid the meat was so vile it would ruin her pan. Notice that no shark recipes made it into her cookbook. But, the shark actually tasted good and the meat we fried up all got eaten quickly. Halibut is much better than shark, but it was an interesting experiment.

After we got all the fish vacuumed packed and sealed, it was about 10 P.M. What made matters worse is we kept overheating the vacuum packer,

Above: Our haul of fish the first day we were out fishing. Not a bad catch!
Below: The three spiny dogfish sharks.

Above: Shane with the salmon he caught. Below left: An illustration of Moses and a halibut. Below right: An illustration of Andrew with his shark.

Halibut   Shark

and then we would have to wait a few minutes for it to cool down. In the future I may need to buy a bigger packer; or simply having a second one of the same size to speed things up.

The next day, Friday, we decided to go fishing again. Everyone was stoked about going out again. Henry even bought another halibut rod at Ulmer's Hardware in Homer. Not wanting to be outdone, I bought another one as well. This gave us four rods, so we figured we would really haul the fish in this time.

Unfortunately, the fishing wasn't as good this time around. Henry's wife, Nancy, was along for this trip. The sea was rough, and it would have taken a long time to get to Seldovia in such rough water. A boat in rough seas not only goes slower, it takes a lot more fuel. I was concerned if we tried to go to Seldovia and back, we would run out of gas. We stayed mostly behind the Spit, and tried fishing several spots. We caught one halibut that day. Whitecaps were everywhere, and multiple times the water sprayed in over the front of the boat, getting us wet. This wasn't enough water to be any threat of swamping the boat, it was just spray. Samuel enjoys bird watching, so we took him past Gull Island, which is home to thousands of sea gulls and other birds. He saw quite a few "lifers." A lifer is not someone who escaped prison, it is a bird you saw for the first time in your life, in the wild. Going to zoos doesn't count, or so I was told.

I couldn't help but be impressed with Marlene. While we were out fishing, she took all the children, packed them in the shot up blue van, and went out berry picking. When we returned from fishing Nancy made a cobbler out of them. The blue van is a 4-speed manual, not to mention a bit of an eyesore. Even though they didn't go far, just out the lane, it proved Marlene is in fact, an Alaskan (not that being a Pennsylvanian is bad).

The following day, Saturday, we decided to give fishing another try. This time the waves were even worse! It made for the most interesting boating I have ever done. At first I was quite worried, and tried to cover it up by making jokes about being scared. But the Lund was amazing; it took the high waves with no problem. We would have been in serious trouble with my smaller 16' skiff. After awhile I started even enjoying myself. You could drive right up the side of the waves. This was a little like surfing, and actually fun, after I realized we were not in any real danger.

Because of our poor success the day before, we decided to try for Seldovia again. We threw an extra gas can in the boat, just in case. But, like the previous day, the seas were so rough we decided to not go the entire distance

Above: The Homer small boat harbor. The water height can vary by 30 feet between low and high tide. Below: Navigating out to the inlet.

to Seldovia. On the way to find a fishing spot we saw whales, closer than I have ever seen them before. This was a real highlight! It is hard to judge the size of the whales in the pictures, but believe me, they were big.

As we were trying to fish, we noticed a charter boat go past. It seemed like a good idea to just follow the charter boat, and fish where they fished. This particular charter didn't fare so well, or else they got mad we were following them and intentionally fished at bad spots. We did catch a few halibut, I believe it was three or four, before heading back to the dock. The fish were caught before we followed the charter. I guess the charter boat should have followed us instead! In some ways, it would have been nice to have the best fishing day last. But I am just glad we had that really good day fishing. In reality, all the days we fished were good.

That week some fellows from Pennsylvania stopped in. It was John Lapp, from the PCBE (Plain Communities Business Exchange), Marlene's cousin Jesse Stauffer, and some others whose names I forget. Inspired by Book 2, they had purchased an enclosed trailer and planned on hauling it to Alaska and reselling it. However, I did neglect to warn about some potential complications with the trailer hauling arrangement. Enclosed trailers are big and heavy and will cut your fuel mileage considerably. Unless you enjoy your vehicle swinging uncontrollably, you have to drive under the speed limit. These fellows discovered this early on in the trip, and were so tired of the trailer slowing them down they left it in Montana!

Drunks Fighting Downstairs!
Chapter 16

After all the fun gold panning, fishing, and touring Alaska, it was time for the Swarey family to head home. Because Henry, being Amish, doesn't fly he had to plan a land route for the entire trip. This involved trains, boats, and even our van. As Henry was planning the trip, he called and asked if we could drop them off in Prince Rupert, Canada. Henry is a good friend, and we would do about anything for their family. Without giving it any thought, I agreed. Marlene tells me I am absent minded at times, and she is probably right. One time, while still living with my parents, I put a pizza in the oven upside down. They still blame me (20 years later) for their oven not working right. Anyway, a little while later I was thinking over this conversation with Henry. Suddenly it occurred to me: He said "Canada!" There is no place, in Canada, close to Anchor Point, Alaska! I checked this on Google maps and discovered the route was 1,762 miles-one way! That is over 33 hours of driving time-one way! We were delighted. It's not every day you get such a long, all expense paid road trip!

We are an easy sell for road trips. One time we drove Marlene's uncle and aunt (Ivan and Anna Martin) to California. Another time we drove to Michigan, just for the fun of it. Then there was trips to Texas, Florida, and who knows where all over the years. There was a small problem with the trip to Prince Rupert. Our flight to Nome was out of Anchorage on the morning of July 24. Thursday evening, July 21 was when we needed to drop Henry's off to catch their train. That left us less than 3 days to make the 1,500 plus mile drive back to Anchorage. After some quick calculations, we realized we would be fine as long as we didn't stop to sleep. More concerning though was the possibility of van breakdowns. Our van had over 200,000 miles on it so it was no longer a "spring chicken." If we missed the plane, then "poof" our trip to Nome was toast. Nonrefundable plane tickets meant they were nonrefundable! Adding insult to injury our motel and rental van were pre-paid. It was pretty important we didn't miss our plane!

Tuesday morning we left Anchor Point around 7 in the morning. Henry had, months before, booked motels along the route. Henry's ability to plan ahead amazes me, and it's a wonder we get along so well. Our first night was to be spent in Tok, Alaska. This is the last town of any size heading to the Canadian border. You may recognize this town from our other books. It is also home to the restaurant "Fast Eddies", which is fine dining in that neck of the woods.

Above: We drove past wildfires along Turnagain Arm, just outside of Anchorage. Below: We saw helicopters pick up water with baskets and dump it on the fire. It was fascinating to watch! It is probably an expensive (but effective) way to fight fires.

Actually, Fast Eddies is good compared to food in more populated areas. Tok is also where we met Jason's family (they lived in Tok and owned two limousines), who later shocked us with the announcement that they decided to become Polygamists. You meet all types of people in Alaska!

We arrived in Tok on schedule, which was around 8 in the evening. I don't remember the name of the motel, but they had sled dogs tied up in the parking lot. Because of the amount of children we had, we reserved two rooms for just our family (some motels require this, and others do not). Shane and myself slept in one room, and Marlene and the girls in the other.

Marlene was woken up that morning by what was obviously drunk people fighting in the room below her. The one kept shouting at the other "You're wrong, and I'm right!" They jumped from topic to topic, and at one point discussed fire. "You don't know anything about fire!" the one man shouted. The other replied, "Yes I do! It's hot!!" And so on. At first Marlene said she expected a real brawl to break out, or maybe even gunshots. But as the argument wore on, it became less and less loud. It did last long enough for me to hear it, when I came over to their room to pickup the luggage.

I was reminded of Proverbs 20:1 "Wine is a mocker, strong drink is raging: and whosoever is deceived thereby is not wise."

Our next stop for that evening was Watson Lake, Yukon. This is home to the "Sign Post Forest," discussed earlier in the book by Josh and mentioned in our other books. We stopped at the Ram's Horn Motel. It was here that I got into trouble with the family. Our arrival was late, after 9 P.M. This meant all the restaurants in town were closed except for one across the parking lot from our motel. I decided to quickly run over and get a menu, bring it back to the family, and let them decide what to pick. Henry's had grabbed some pizza at the gas station, but for whatever reason we did not. I think by the time we checked in our room, the gas station closed, or maybe Henry's cleaned out the pizza. I don't remember.

When I walked in the restaurant, they announced they were closing in a few minutes, but I could squeak in an order. This left no time for me to run back out and check what the family wanted. One of my weak points is predicting my families palate. It's not that they are so unpredictable, it's just that when there is food around I pay more attention to it than I should, and less attention to the family. With eight people the preferences run across the entire spectrum. That evening I decided to play it safe and order hamburgers. Sure enough, nobody wanted hamburgers that evening.

The next day, in the late afternoon, we arrived in Prince Rupert. After dropping the Swarey family off at their motel, we headed over to

Above: Sled dogs at the hotel (same one with the drunks), tied up outside the pickup truck with the dog boxes and sled on the back. Below: The children all posed for pictures along the road with wild flowers, except Mary Kate insisted on looking the wrong way!

McDonald's and grabbed a quick meal. One thing I have noticed is McDonald's are considerably nicer in Canada. They are cleaner, serve poutine, and have touch screens to order. They have other menu items not available in the U.S., but no unsweetened tea. If you order unsweetened tea you get blank looks from the clerk, and no options on the touch screen.

Then it was a mad dash back to Anchorage. Thinking back, I can't remember much from the return trip. I remember being tired a lot, and feeling rather grimy. Marlene is a real diehard when it comes to driving. She can drive all night and then some. I'm not quite so durable. We made it to Anchorage in good time, arriving Saturday in the early afternoon.

That afternoon Missie and some of the Yoder family met us at our motel with the motorhome. Our durable, good motorhome, not the Mallard, which had already long been traded for the boat. Missie was to fly to Nome with us, and the Yoder's would take our van back to Sterling, where we would later pick it up. So why did we need the motorhome? Were we planning to drive it to Nome? No...after returning from Nome, we planned to jump in the motorhome and head south again! Proof that we are just not right in the head. We had some business to attend to in Ohio, and Desiree wanted to go to camp. I should have called this book "The Year of Much Driving!" While in Nome, the motorhome would be parked at the nearby Airport Parking storage lot, where it took up multiple parking spaces and racked up a hefty bill.

Left to right: Sylvester Yoder, Savilla Yoder, Ervin Yoder, and Missie Sauder. Could anyone in this picture explain Missie's haste to return from Fairbanks to Sterling?

Arrested at the Airport
Chapter 17

Sunday morning dawned bright and clear. We regretted not being able to go to church that Sunday, but sometimes when you travel you have to fit the plane's schedule. We took the motel's shuttle to the airport, as we had already parked the motorhome at the Airport Parking Lot the night before. That is capitalized, because it is actually the name of the business, for all you people that love to go through and count typos. I was worried we would end up being late, but everything went smoothly, and we were at the airport in plenty of time.

The last time we flew on a commercial airline we had one child, Shane. He was a year and a half old. We quickly discovered flying got a lot more complicated with seven children! As we were (slowly) making our way through the security line, Dallas had a "blowout." For those of you not familiar with child care, this is an unpleasant condition involving the diaper contents ending up on the outside of the diaper! Naturally they occur at inconvenient moments.

Airports have X-ray scanners that you need to put your luggage, purses, etc, through. The machines then scan the items, giving the people watching the screen an idea of what is inside your stuff. As I was approaching the scanners I noticed a large sign saying "No power tools in your carry on." This worried me a little bit, as I kept the camera in a Makita bag. The bag used to house a cordless Makita drill, but it had moved on to other pastures. The stiff walls and padded sides made it a great camera case. The lady running the scanner looked like she had escaped from a library somewhere. Librarians make me nervous, always fretting over that crazy Dewey decimal system.

Sure enough, as soon as my camera bag went through the scanner, the librarian lady started looking really upset. "Oh boy, here it goes," I thought. I mentally prepared a good explanation of why I was using a power tool case for my camera. The stern looking lady didn't even mention power tools though. "Is that there your bag!" she snapped. Concerned, I confirmed it was. "Is there any thing harmful or dangerous in here?" she snarled. "No, just my camera," I replied, all the while thinking this woman was a shade dull.

With sudden gusto, the lady unzipped the case and pulled out a box of bullets. Not just any bullets, but my .454 Casull bear loads. Uh oh. There was no way this could end well. With a terrible, sinking feeling, I suddenly remembered I had put them in there the week before when we went hiking.

"Then what are these?" she said with an air of triumph. I was speechless. "Uh, uh, uh," was all I could muster. Another security agent quickly ran over. "Wow, some heavy hitters!" he exclaimed. This was not what I wanted to hear. I feebly offered my explanation, feeling like someone who had just gotten busted driving 120 mph through a school zone, on the wrong side of the road, with children strapped on the roof. "We'll have to call the state police," said the second agent, who at least appeared a bit friendlier than the deranged librarian.

Marlene had just returned from cleaning up Dallas, and was not at all amused by the situation. It wasn't very unusual for her to find bullets in the washing machine, and she seemed under the impression I was not very organized with my ammunition. We had to wait around for the police to show up, which was somewhat embarrassing. I hoped I would still get to Nome, and not end up in the local police station. I guess standing there with our seven children I didn't look like a terrorist, because the police officer who arrived seemed jovial. "This happens all the time," he said. "I can see this was just a mistake." He then wrote down my name, address, and a bunch of other information. At that point he even offered the bullets back, provided I checked it into my luggage, and did not take it on my carry on. We had already checked our luggage in, so I declined and told the officer he could just keep the bullets. He seemed pleased by this.

Finally, we cleared the security check point and gathered everyone at the gate. Even with the security delay, we were still very early. To board the plane we needed to walk outside on the runway. The children were excited about flying and couldn't wait to experience the take off. Mary Kate is scared of loud noises, so I was a bit concerned what her reaction would be. Before a jet takes off, they put their wheel brakes on, and rev the engines. After some time they release the brakes, and the sensation of acceleration is amazing. The take off speed for a full size jet is around 150 mph.

Mary Kate did in fact panic as the plane left the ground. The combination of the speed, noise, and other ruckus was too much for her. I wasn't sure what to do, but Marlene had the situation well under control. She pulled out a pacifier and gave it to Mary Kate, and that was the end of that. She fell asleep quickly! A few months before we had taken her "nuk" but she still liked to steal Dallas's.

The flight to Nome from Anchorage is about an hour and a half. Direct by air it is 540 miles. On ground by dog sled it is over 1,000 miles. By road it is...wait there is no road! The only reason you can travel it by dog sled is because the rivers freeze over and can then be used for a highway.

U.S. Department of Homeland Security
Special Enforcement Program Office (TSA-801)
601 S. 12th Street
Arlington, VA 20598-6801

WARNING NOTICE
Case No. 201█████████

October 7, 2016

Matthew Snader
PO Box 988
Anchor Point, AK 99556

Dear Matthew Snader:

On or about July 24, 2016, while you were at Ted Stevens Anchorage International Airport, you presented yourself and your accessible property for inspection. On that date, during the screening process, the following item(s) were discovered: **Part(s) of Firearm(s) and/or Ammunition.** Your possession of this item(s) violates 1540.111(a) Carriage of weapons, explosives, and incendiaries by individuals (Person). of the Transportation Security Regulations.

Items such as these are not allowed on board an aircraft or in the sterile area of the airport without authorization. Bringing prohibited items to the security screening checkpoint, even accidentally, lengthens the security screening process, violates federal regulations and may, in serious or repeat cases, result in monetary penalties and/or criminal prosecution. A list of permitted and prohibited items is available at www.tsa.gov. Please check this list prior to arrival at the airport.

At this time the Transportation Security Administration has determined that this Warning Notice adequately addresses this incident and no further action is required on your part. We appreciate your future compliance with all security measures.

Please note that this civil penalty action is separate from any other federal, state or local criminal proceeding that may have been brought against you. Resolution of this civil penalty action will not resolve any such criminal proceeding. Similarly, resolution of any criminal proceedings that may have been instituted against you, will not resolve this civil penalty action.

Individuals may be disqualified from TSA Pre✓® screening because they have committed a violation of a TSA security regulation. These violations include (but are not limited to) possession of a prohibited item at a screening location. The TSA Pre✓® disqualification process is separate from this regulatory matter and is handled by a different office. Individuals with questions concerning their TSA Pre✓® status should contact the TSA Contact Center at (866) 289-9673.

If you have questions or comments about this letter, please write to us via email at NOV.APO@dhs.gov . However, if you are unable to contact TSA through this method you may also write to this office at the below address:

DHS/TSA
Special Enforcement Program Office (TSA-801)
601 S. 12th Street
Arlington, VA 20598-6801

Sincerely,

S. Carrera
Aviation Compliance, Branch Manager
Office of Security Operations
U.S. Department of Homeland Security/ TSA

Many people are disappointed when they visit Alaska. They land in Anchorage, look out the window, and see civilization! If it was not for the mountains in the background, and the occasional moose running down the street, it would look just like many other cities in the lower 48. Nome is not this way. When you land in Nome, you realize that you are definitely not in the lower 48 anymore.

The Nome airport didn't look like much. It seemed like they just threw a pole building at the end of the runway, and that was about it. There was a chain link fence around the runway, but it didn't look strong or high enough to keep terrorists from jumping over it and stealing planes. They probably don't have many terrorists around Nome anyway.

I had been told there would be taxis out front for hire, but the taxis all drove off with other customers leaving us standing there, looking around bewildered. Finally I called the visitor's center, and a fellow named Leon answered. I told him of our sad plight, and he that said he would send out a taxi, A.S.A.P. And sure enough, a few minutes later one showed up!

On the way to the motel we passed the famous "burled arch", which announces the finish line of the Iditarod. Every March this is put on main street, and mushers cross through it to finish the 1,000 mile dog sled race from Anchorage. Think about it- 1,000 miles across the frozen interior of Alaska on a dog sled! What could be more fun?

For $20 the taxi took us a mile and a half to our motel, the Aurora Inn. I had randomly picked one, and it did seem like I had happened across a good one. Unlike most of the prices in Nome, lodging is actually fairly reasonable. Vehicle rentals are priced pretty good too, considering they all need to be barged in. We had an F-350 van lined up, that I had reserved several months before. When we checked in at the motel I asked about the van. They told me the van was out front, with the keys in the ignition. When I expressed surprise that they would do this, they replied, "If someone stole the van, where would they go with it?"

One thing I was not impressed with was our rental van's tires. It seemed the tires were all at the very tail end of their lifecycle. The front fender was also beat up, so the door hardly opened. Overall the van was in good shape, except it had no spare tire! I told the front desk that I must have a spare tire, and they gave me one without any hesitation. Nome has three

Above: Nome has no fancy little halls that connect to the plane.
Below: The plane is reflected in the windows of the terminal.

roads that lead out from it. We planned to explore all of these, and the longest one is about 90 miles long. It would be a pickle to have a flat tire that far out of Nome. If you have a flat outside of Nome, you're on your own!

The Roads from Nome

There are three roads that lead out of Nome. They are as follows:

1. Nome to Teller

Teller is a small Native American (Inupiat) town, about 73 miles from Nome. Teller is only 55 miles from Russia! At one point Teller had over 5,000 residents but is now down to less than 300 people. It was originally a gold rush town but the residents now live on subsistence living, although it does sound like some gold prospecting still goes on there.

2. Nome – Taylor Road

The Taylor road goes about 85 miles outside of Nome and ends at a dilapidated bridge.

3. Nome to Council

Council is a ghost town 72 miles outside of Nome. The entire town is privately owned, so unfortunately you can't just wander around it. Council is older than Nome. The "3 Lucky Swedes" who discovered gold in Anvil Creek originally started out at Council. There are 30 or 40 people who still live here, way down from the peak of 15,000 in the heydays of the gold rush. The famous "trains to nowhere" are along this route. Also on this route is the Safety Roadhouse, the last checkpoint in the Iditarod.

Photo used from Wikipedia, public domain.

Above: Playing in the Bering Sea-not much is more refreshing than 40 degree water!
Below: Nome with the manmade granite wall to keep the ocean out.

The Taylor Road
Chapter 19

On our first day at Nome we didn't do much (it was Sunday). We walked down to the famous beach which no longer has "golden sands." That didn't stop me from trying my hand at gold panning anyway (is playing with a gold pan work?). This seemed to amuse the locals that I talked to.

The beach is lined with a man-made granite wall. Prior to the wall being constructed, storms would occasionally wash half the town away. Nome has no natural barrier to protect it from the ocean, causing many problems in the olden days. It seemed if Nome wasn't burning down or freezing up, it was flooding out or washing away.

After getting our spare tire, I was chomping at the bit to do some sight seeing. After all, it's not every day you get to see Nome! One of the locals I talked to had sounded alarmed when I informed him we did not bring any firearms along. Nome doesn't have any trees, and I figured wildlife would be in short supply. No trees, no bears, I figured. Or if you did see a bear, you can see it miles away, and easily avoid it. This particular local decided to educate me on bears, and even told me that we could run across the dreaded Polar bears. Polar bears are the only known animal to actively hunt humans. Sure, the other bears will sometimes have a quick bite or two but they don't consider humans a really genuine food source. But Polar bears consider humans right up there with seals and fish. After discussing the merits of getting eaten, I decided to go down to the local gun shop and pickup a 12 gauge. After all, sales were probably down, and they needed some help anyway. The next day, Monday, we set out to find the gun shop.

Finding the gun shop took more work than I expected. With the van packed and everyone loaded, we drove to the address wher the gun shop was supposed to be. No gun shop. After talking to a local, he pointed us to the other side of town. Nome isn't very big, so in three minutes we drove past where the gun shop should have been. Still no gun shop! After some close examination, we discovered a building with moose antlers nailed to it. Under the antlers was some faded writing that seemed to indicate it might be a store.

Shane and I cautiously entered the building, and sure enough it was a gun shop. One thing we quickly discovered about Nome is that most buildings look rather worn out on the outside but are much nicer on the inside. Perhaps the arctic weather makes them look that way. Maybe that's just fashion in the far north. First I checked to see if they had bear spray, but I was told they were sold out. I was then pleased to discover the gun shop

Nome's finest gun shop (and the only I could find). I would include the name, but I can't read the did have a fairly decent selection of guns. There was a 12 gauge pump action Mossburg "Maverick" for sale, very similar to the one we have named "Mabel." It was priced at $299, which wasn't bad for Nome. I told the friendly salesman we would take it, and proceeded to fill out the paperwork. Even in Nome, Alaska you need a background check to buy a gun from a gun shop. I'm not saying this is good or bad, just pointing it out.

As I was filling out the gun purchaser forms a fellow walked in and said he needed to buy some 12 gauge slugs. "We are all out," the salesman said. This got my attention. A shot gun without slugs is not very good bear protection. The fellow then asked if they had buckshot available. "All we have is this," said the salesman, pulling out some bird shot. Bird shot is not suitable, at all, for shooting bears. I stopped filling out the paperwork and told the salesman that I didn't want his shotgun after all, explaining that I wanted it for bear protection. "The slugs should be in next month," the salesman said helpfully. Except this didn't help us at all.

Noticing they also had some rifles, I asked about them. "Got a nice 30.06 right here," he said. I always wanted to try a 30.06, so I thought it over. Then came the kicker. "Except I don't have any bullets for it." I asked what guns he did actually have bullets for, and this narrowed the selection down quite a bit. All these guns were over $600, way too much to just buy anyhow. He had some handguns, but no .454's. Finally I gave up, and said I decided not to buy anything. As I left, the salesman kept reminding me how unpleasant it was to get mauled by bears. Had I bought a gun, I would have also needed to buy a good airline approved gun case to ship it back on the airplane. They probably would have been out of them as well. After awhile it's easier to just get chased around by bears.

Finally we were on the road to check out the Taylor highway, with no guns or bear spray. We decided we would just have to stick close to the vehicle. Marlene suggested this all was possibly a ruse to buy another a gun. What funny notions women don't come up with.

The first highlight on the Taylor highway was a herd of Musk Ox. Only a mile or two outside of town we came across a herd. They are very funny, hairy looking things. They seem pretty lazy and don't move very fast, but there was a little baby with the herd that did. This struck Mary Kate's fancy, and she kept shouting "Baby musk ox!" and pointing. Of course hearing a two year old shout this is much cuter than me shouting it.

I was surprised how many buildings were along the highway. I did notice the further we got from town, the more run down they looked,

Above: Inside Nome's only gun shop.
Below: Musk Ox in someone's back yard, just outside of Nome.

Above: A fine looking yurt outside Nome. Below: The children pick berries along the road.

generally. There were some nice houses way out of town. We also saw several yurts. They are round, tent like structures. I think they originated in Mongolia, but somehow Alaskans took a fancy to them.

Along the highway we also discovered berry bushes. We had fun hiking a little bit beside the road and finding berries. There were no trees at all. We saw another herd of musk ox further away. I took the drone up and tried to get out to them, but I kept getting "out of range" messages before I could get close enough for good pictures. Along the road is quite a bit of old equipment—rusted out steam shovels, sluices, and who knows what.

The road ends at a bridge with a :road closed" sign. I greatly wondered what was on the other side of the bridge, as obviously the road used to go somewhere or they wouldn't have put a bridge there. But the bridge had huge holes in the floor, and I don't think we could have even gotten the van across. I doubt the van rental company would have been really happy with us had we fallen through the bridge with their van.

On the way back to Nome I tried again to take pictures of the musk ox herd. This time ended in near disaster for the drone. A high wind was blowing across the road, which was directly beside a steep ravine. The musk ox were down at the bottom of the ravine. It did occur to me that it might be too windy for flying, but I didn't give it a lot of thought. As the drone took off and hovered at the four foot level, it acted like I was accelerating it backwards. But I wasn't touching the controls! And it was heading right for the ravine, being pushed by the wind. I could have probably fought the wind and flew it back under full power, but I'm not really that good at flying. Instead I ran after the drone and grabbed it before the wind pushed it out over the ravine, and in the process I dropped my phone and cracked the screen.

It was no loss to crack my phone screen, as I affectionately called this particular phone "Benedict Arnold." It would randomly call people. I figured this must have been because I bumped it in my pocket, but once I had it laying in front of me on my desk. All at once it dialed a random number on my contact list! Nothing was close to it. To top it off, the phone must have been jealous of the drone, because later it formatted the memory card (I used it for a little after Nome with the cracked screen) in the phone, destroying some of my Nome photos! Sometimes it's just better to cut your losses.

We made it back to Nome with no problems. Later that evening I ran out for some gas, which I found for $5 a gallon! I also stopped at the grocery store, and upon coming out, discovered I had a flat tire! Thankful I had a spare, I jacked up the van and proceeded to change the tire. A fellow parked

Above: The end of the line. Below: Some of the equipment you see scattered over the countryside.

beside me commented he just had a flat, but it happened far out of town and he didn't have a spare tire. When I asked what he did, he said he just drove back to town on the rim!

The next day (July 26) we decided to sit tight and just walk around Nome. We were scheduled to be there a whole week, and there are only three roads out of Nome. This left several spare days to check out the local sights. The visitor's center was only a mile, or less, from the motel so we decided to head down there and check it out.

We also figured it would be a good day to take pictures in front of the burled arch, as the Iditarod sign is called. However, as we walked down main street, the burled arch was missing! My motto is "strike while the iron is hot", and we should not have hesitated to take the pictures as soon as we arrived. The arch is a well known landmark in Alaska, and not getting a picture of it would be a real letdown.

At the visitor's center we met the fellow, Leon, that I had talked to the day we arrived, and summoned a taxi for us. Leon lived in Nome year round, and was full of helpful information. We discussed many interesting topics, including Musk Ox, the Iditarod, and house construction. Leon described watching mushers coming in to finish the Iditarod.

Nome is built on permafrost. I asked Leon how people build on permafrost, as this is what causes the road to heave and gives all sorts of stability problems. Permafrost is frozen ground. As long as it remains frozen, it is solid as a rock. If it melts, it turns to mud. What keeps permafrost from melting is the insulated tundra above it. The Trans-Alaska pipeline is mounted on a foundation of refrigerated pilings. A system like that is expensive, and while some of the more elaborate buildings have refrigerated foundations, most do not.

Leon explained there were several ways to build a house on permafrost. One method was to dig a deep pit, fill it with gravel, and build on top of it. The gravel would hopefully keep the ground frozen underneath. Another method was to simply build on piers, or cement blocks, the way our Alaska house is built. Keeping an open airspace between the ground and house helped keep the ground from thawing out. If it did thaw a little, you could always jack up the house and re-level it. "So is it like a spring ritual to level out your house?" I asked Leon. He replied "No, it is more like once every decade or two, when dishes start falling out of the cupboards." I thought of my own house in Anchor Point. Despite the dire predictions of Pennsylvania builders, who nearly had aneurisms when seeing pictures of my pier blocks sitting on a gravel pad, it is still level and hasn't moved. But I didn't build on permafrost either.

Above: A house built with a sophisticated adjustable foundation system.
Below: This flag was hanging in the town center of Nome.

I also asked Leon about the missing Iditarod sign. He paused, as if in deep thought. "Well," he said. "The official reason it was removed was to be touched up and refinished." Ok, I thought, that sounds reasonable. But then Leon added, "But rumor has it that the sign was put away because it was announced on Facebook that a bunch of Hillary supporters were going to take a campaign picture in front of it." Now, these books aren't meant to be political in nature, so we won't make comments about presidential campaigns. I was a bit surprised to hear there were any Hillary supporters around, as Alaskans are generally very hardworking, decent, pro-gun, pro-energy, and pro-freedom. Of course, they might have been tourists, or maybe even escaped convicts hiding from the law.

Since statehood in 1959, Alaska has only gone for one Democratic candidate, Lyndon B. Johnson. (Editors note: Trump took Alaska by 52.9% of the vote, compared to Hillary's 37.7% in the 2016 presidential election.) Alaska only has 3 electoral votes, so it's not really a dominant player in national elections. It takes 270 electoral votes to win the race for the White House.

Hillary or not, this missing sign caused some concern on my part. Being an Iditarod fan, and having actually named my youngest son after the 4 time Iditarod champion Dallas Seavey, I wanted pretty badly to see the burled arch. I asked Leon if there was any chance of contacting the officials in charge of the sign. He said this was a possibility, demonstrating something I love about the Iditarod dog sled race.

In Alaska, the Iditarod is basically as popular as NASCAR, the NFL, and the Olympics combined. The race routinely makes headlines on all major papers and news networks in the state. Despite this, I have talked to several Iditarod mushers on their personal cell phones, including twice champion Mitch Seavey. Try that with NASCAR drivers or star football players! It may not be impossible, but I bet it is pretty difficult. You want to compete in NASCAR? I hope you have several million dollars of liquid capital ready to burn. Want to buy a football team? I'm pretty sure they cost a lot more than a dog sled team! And you can't just feed them frozen salmon to keep them happy.

Running the Iditarod is no picnic or walk in the park. However, if you have a real fire in your belly, you could probably do it. Yes, it would take thousands of dollars (but not millions) and a lot of time and practice, but you could probably pull it off. There is a story about a guy who caught Iditarod fever and emptied out the dog pound in Anchorage to run it. I'm pretty sure he didn't win, and I don't know if he even finished. But the point is you

Above: The streets of Nome. Below: Check out those gas prices! Nome is also called "Anvil City" hence the name for the gas station.

can't drag a rusty old Crown Victoria out of the weeds and head down to the NASCAR track and compete.

After a pleasant visit at the visitor's center, we took a walk around the town. On one street we encountered a woman who had obviously been drinking. She kept asking me for a hug (of all things!), and I told her Marlene would be happy to give her a hug. So Marlene gave the poor lady a hug, but she kept asking me again for a hug. I'm not in the habit of hugging strange ladies on the street, so I let her hug Dallas instead. She seemed ok with that. We talked with her a little bit. It seemed like she had a sad home situation.

One funny thing Mary Kate did at the motel was take her shoes off every time we went inside the motel. She must have thought the motel was a house, and the motel rooms bedrooms.

After we got back to the hotel I talked to some fellows who were hanging around the porch. I asked them what they do all day, and they said they didn't have anything to do but drink. Bars and Saloons in town seem to outnumber all the other establishments combined. Nome has been called "sin city" for more reasons than just alcohol. Thankfully, I did notice several churches in Nome, however most of them seemed to be closed. If you're reading this book, and your church or congregation is struggling with where to plan the next outreach, maybe you should consider Nome. We are currently involved in starting a new church plant in Alaska (Clam Gulch/Kasilof area) in 2017, and part of the planning is to decide where to put an outreach in 10 years. Maybe Nome? Maybe not-time will tell!

If we do start an outreach in Nome, or some other remote town in Alaska, what might be a good tool for the outreach? Why, airplanes, of course. And what do you need to fly an airplane? A pilot's license! These are things I need to keep in mind. Hopefully I plan ahead and don't put things off until the last minute. One of our church members also happens to be a flight instructor.

Above: The Aurora Inn, where we stayed. Below: Aerial shot of Nome. The motel is in the center, right behind the road closest to the camera.

The Road to Council, and the Trains to Nowhere
Chapter 20

Wednesday, July 27, was my birthday. What better way to celebrate a birthday than a road trip out of Nome? We topped off the tank with some $5 a gallon gasoline and headed out of town. Shane seemed to think these road trips were torture. He usually reads when we drive, but because we flew into Nome, he couldn't drag dozens of books along. I had trouble feeling any sympathy when he said most other boys his age weren't forced to ride around Nome. I told him he must be spoiled.

Our destination was the ghost town of Council. This town is located 73 miles from Nome, accessible by the Nome-Council Road. Council existed before Nome, where the "Three Lucky Swedes" went first to pan for gold. They left because all the good spots were claimed. Later they found gold in the Anvil Creek and never looked back. Nome was founded on the banks of the Anvil Creek.

The first part of the drive was along the banks of the Bering Sea, east out of Nome. We were following the route of the last leg of the Iditarod (although going the wrong direction), and around mile 30 the Safety Roadhouse came into view. This is the last checkpoint of the race, also known as "Port Safety." We kept going, but decided we would stop in on the way back from Council.

At around Mile 33 we came to the famous "Trains to Nowhere". The poor guys that hauled these trains here. If you think it's a sad tale of woe to haul a large, ugly, defective boat to Alaska (which it is) then you have to hear this story. In the mid 1800's New York City developed an elevated train system using Forney steam locomotives. As time progressed they decided to replace these engines with lighter, cleaner electric ones. They sold the old steam engines at fire sale prices to whoever wanted them. In 1903 investors bought three of these engines and hauled them to Nome. Imagine transporting steam locomotives for thousands of miles in 1903. Their idea was to connect Nome to Council, and service the mining camps in the area. Certainly this was a good sounding idea.

Like many good sounding ideas, this didn't translate so well into real life. I have had personal experience with ideas like this. Thankfully, Marlene helps me sort these ideas out. I'm pretty sure she would have shot down the idea of barging huge, heavy locomotives to Alaska. Turns out getting trains to Alaska was the least of the investors' problems. Did you ever price installing railroads over permafrost?

Above: A herd of Musk Ox. Allegedly they can be aggressive, but these seemed pretty laid back. Below: The Trains to Nowhere!

Above and Below: The Trains to Nowhere! These trains were hauled the whole way from New York City, over a century ago. I should have brought some coal along, I could have tried to fire one up.

The investors actually did get a railroad going for a time. They started the *Council City and Solomon River Railroad*. They did run the trains and haul freight. But in 1913 a storm destroyed the Solomon River Railroad bridge, and the trains were stranded. One hundred and three years later we showed up and took some pictures of them. They are very rusty now, as the trains are over 130 years old. One cool thing about Nome is that you can walk up and sit on these trains if you want. A historical site like this in the lower 48 would probably have armed guards stationed around it.

After the trains we continued on to Council. I was hoping to be able to run around the ghost town and explore old buildings. However, before we could get into the town, a large sign warned us that the entire town was private property. It was obvious they didn't want people there fooling around. Later I read that 30 or 40 families actually still live there, which to me doesn't seem to be a legitimate ghost town. If fact, I struggled with feeling a little jealous. How neat would it be to have your own private town?

On the way back to Nome we decided to stop and take some pictures of an antique gold dredge. I'm not sure how old this particular one is, but I was told the last dredge quit in the 1980's. This dredge seemed to be quite a bit older than that. The belt with scoops would bite into the dirt, bring scoopfuls back into the dredge, where the material would be sorted, then the dirt would be discarded behind the dredge. Slowly the dredge would move across the landscape, floating in a pond that moved with it. Many of the dredges were steam powered.

The dredge machines did tear up the landscape, leaving piles of debris behind them. This did thaw out the top layers of permafrost, causing the ground to eventually become more stable. One fringe benefit of dredging is that it creates large swathes of thawed out, stable, piles of ground. The Nome airport is built on these dredge pilings.

After the dredge we came back to the Safety Roadhouse. I had assumed this would be a tourist trap, piled full of crowds of people. After all, who wouldn't want to come to Nome and see the last checkpoint of the Iditarod? But surprisingly, nobody seemed to be there. We poked around inside, rather intrigued by the $1 bills glued all over the walls. Finally we heard someone holler from the back, and a fellow came out to talk to us. When I inquired about getting some food, he mentioned something about maybe he could find some hot dogs in the freezer. This wasn't quite what we had in mind, so I told him we were just sight seeing. Apparently this wasn't their peak tourist time. I'm sure in March they are much busier.

Above: Aerial photo looking towards Council. Below: Looking away from Council.

It was fascinating to see a place wallpapered with money. People often leave notes, sign their name, etc, on $1 bills and fasten them to the wall. The fellow there said that last time he counted the bills he gave up at 8,000. He said the problem with this arrangement is that if they decided to remodel anything, people get upset if you take "their" money down. If I owned the place, I think I would do an annual spring cleaning, and haul all the wall paper to the bank! But that may end the tradition. I liked the décor so much, I'm thinking about redoing my office in a similar fashion. However I think I'll used cashed checks that I deposited remotely instead of $1 bills. Or, maybe I'll use Iraqi dinars (dollars). Nine dollars US will buy you over 10,000 Iraqi dinars. That is probably even cheaper than regular wallpaper! In fact, it would seem like the Iraqi mint might lose money on printing. Speaking of which: Sometimes people ask what kind of money we use in Alaska! Hint: What nation is Alaska part of?

We made it back to Nome without incident, which left us the road to Teller to explore yet.

Since it was my birthday, we left the children in Missie's care and headed over to Airport Pizza for a date. Nome has several restaurants and this was one of our favorites. We placed our orders and were told "We don't have that in stock." After going through several options, we both found something that was in stock. This is one thing about Nome. Just like in the gun shop, many stores are often out of things. Replacement stock comes by barge, which can take weeks. Of course air transport is available, but shipping anything by air is expensive.

The following day was Thursday, July 28. This is Desiree's birthday; she missed my birthday by 15 minutes. The nurses said we could list July 27 as the birth date anyway, but that just felt a bit cheesy. If we did that, every time we told someone Desiree's birthday, we would always have to add that bit of trivia or feel like we were misleading people. Starting your life off with a lie just doesn't seem like the best start.

For Desiree's birthday we bought a chocolate cake with strawberry icing. Unlike many things in Nome, the cake was reasonably priced. We made some fresh lemonade with real lemons, and unlike the cake, this was a bit pricey. The cost of the ingredients, to make one gallon, cost over $12! You can find this recipe in Marlene's cookbook. Normally it doesn't cost but a fraction of that.

This same day we had a medical incident to deal with. You may remember me mentioning that "my children love nothing better than hurting themselves," although when one of the children heard me say that they disagreed.

Anyway, Lana was swinging between the sofa and the chair by her elbows, when suddenly clunk! She was on the floor, followed by loud, hysterical shrieking. This was despite her being told specifically a few minutes prior not to swing on the furniture. It is not very unusual to hear clunking, banging sounds followed by cries of distress, so I didn't even pay it much thought. However when Marlene gasped and made an excited comment about "blood everywhere" it got my attention.

Somehow, Lana had managed to fall on her head, cutting her ear neatly across the outside of the ear. Given how much a gallon of lemonade cost, I could only imagine how much medical care in Nome might be. I resigned myself to the thought that the cost of the trip had just doubled, and hoped the clinic would accept credit cards. I also did a quick calculation of how much equity we had in our house.

Thankfully, Marlene suggested a calmer approach, and I quickly went out and bought some butterfly bandages and gauze at Safeway. This seemed to work, and the bleeding stopped. A crisis averted! And we did get to have our date anyway, just a bit delayed.

Missie and the girls in the one motel room. Left to right: Lana, Missie, Mary Kate, Kallia, Samantha

Right: Desiree with her birthday cake in our motel room in Nome. Below: Shane holds our $12 gallon lemonade. A large part of the cost was spring water, which is very expensive. They must ship it all in.

The Road to Teller
Chapter 21

Teller is a small Inupiat town located about 70 miles outside of Nome. With a population of less than 300 people, Teller is a small town situated next to the Bering Sea. It is the only actual town you can drive to from Nome, as all the other roads lead to a dead end or ghost town. Teller is only 55 miles from Russia, which is about as close as you can get without a passport. In fact, there used to be a string of early warning radio towers along the coast here. In the event Soviet bombers crossed over they would alert the lower 48. These were called "White Alice" sites, and were used to relay information up to 200 miles apart. After satellites became more developed these sites were discontinued and torn down. Ironically, it was probably safer to be in Teller than the lower 48, as the Soviets would have gotten fallout from their own bombs had they dropped them there.

Despite being the biggest town in the area, Nome is the youngest. The town of Council was established before Nome, and Teller was already being used by the Inupiat natives as a fish camp in 1825. Western Union employees scouted the area and spent the winter there in 1866 and 1867. Later the United States government experimented with importing reindeer, and a reindeer station existed there from 1892 to 1900. In fact, the reindeer story is a fascinating one. In the late 1800's many Inuit people in Alaska were starving because of commercial overfishing of whales. The US government decided to import reindeer from Norway to supplement the Inuit's diet and give them something to raise.

A savvy businessman named Carl Lomen decided that reindeer needed more publicity to become popular as table fare. He engineered several advertisements featuring Santa Claus in a flying sled pulled by reindeer (I'm not sure how Santa supposedly traveled before this). He even went as far as to fake letters from children to the editors of major newspapers around the country asking about "Santa and his reindeer." This advertisement scheme seemed to backfire, as most people now know of "Santa and his reindeer" but eating reindeer is a novelty. In fact, featuring reindeer as lovable creatures pulling Santa's sleigh probably wasn't a good thing to inspire people to slaughter and eat more reindeer. My recommendation to Carl would have been to feature a team of beef cattle pulling the sleigh!

We left for Teller on Desiree's birthday, Thursday, July 28. On the way to Teller we passed a herd of musk ox. It was becoming apparent that there were a lot of musk ox around, and Marlene commented that she would

Above: The town of Teller sits on a spit extending out into the Bering Sea. Below: Boats are an important part of a subsistence lifestyle.

A Native lady named "Elsie" selling handicrafts. The purse is made of sealskin, and many of the other items from bone or tusk. The beadwork is very intricate.

like to hunt them. Unfortunately musk ox tags are issued by drawing, and are very hard to get. That isn't all bad. If everyone started shooting the musk ox I don't think they would last very long. But, it is very rare that Marlene says she would like to hunt something other than drones, so I made a mental note to see what could be done in the future to make this come to pass.

The weather was a bit on the rainy side, but it wasn't too bad. It was chilly, but I think it is usually chilly around Nome. As we drove down the hill into Teller, the town was even smaller than I expected. It was located on what looked like a spit, sticking out into the Bering Sea.

As we drove through the town, it was neat to see racks of drying salmon. With an average annual income of $30,000 the residents have to live a subsistence lifestyle. This means that the average resident does a lot of fishing and hunting. They really have no choice, as anything "bought" here is very expensive. A small box of dog biscuits was $25 at the local store. This is not because the store is run by swindlers, but rather because everything must be shipped in. Prices are already expensive in Nome, and having to haul everything out to Teller doesn't help, not to mention the fact the only store in town is small and probably doesn't buy enormous quantities.

We explored the roads around Teller, which didn't take long. There were quite a few boats, and it was obvious which building was used for power generation. It had about a dozen smoke stacks sticking out the top for various generators.

At the (only) store in Teller we met a local lady named Elsie selling handicrafts. She had a purse made out of seal skin, and quite a few things made with bead work, including walrus tusk. We bought a butterfly from her as a souvenir. The girls wanted to buy everything she had, but since everything is handmade it is also higher priced, so I had to say "no" to that. Natives are the only ones allowed to shoot walruses and seals, so the only way to get souvenirs like this is from a native.

I also met a fellow named Tadd at the store. When I asked him if he ever was along to harpoon whales, he nodded in the affirmative. He wasn't very talkative, or I would have probably grilled him with questions all day. Tadd did describe a little bit of a normal whale hunt. First, you harpoon the whale with an exploding harpoon. He explained it would usually take three harpoons to kill a whale. Honestly, I would be somewhat reluctant to ride around on a little skiff throwing exploding harpoons at whales, but it seemed

Above: Dog biscuits $25.00 Below: Shampoo $9.00

Above: Loaf of white bread $4.05
Below: 18 eggs for $8.10

like something he enjoyed. Actually, I would probably try it if given half the chance.

Tadd also explained how to hunt walrus, seals, sea lions, and polar bears. As far as I am aware, only natives can hunt these animals in the United States. He also had some seal mittens for sale, which I was interested in. The problem was the pair was split up and in two separate locations, both which were not close by. Maybe it's good he didn't run a shoe store. Unfortunately they could not get both the mittens before we left Nome, so I never did get seal skin mittens.

On the way back we again found the musk ox herd. We stopped to watch them, and I launched the drone to get some pictures. They wandered off over a knob, and I followed at a safe distance with the drone. I think it is highly illegal to disturb wildlife with drones. It is also illegal to fly a drone without keeping visual contact (the controller has a live video feed so you can see where you're going without visual contact), and I lost sight of it behind the knob. As I maneuvered it around, trying to get it back into sight, I almost crashed into a bank. It was then that I realized the altitude showed -4 feet. Of course this didn't mean I was underground, but it did mean the drone was four feet lower than the controller. It was high time to get out of there, so I flew straight up to 300 feet and brought it back.

The rest of the drive back to Nome was uneventful. We did stop and explore an abandoned gold dredge beside a creek. Unlike the other one, this one you could walk up to. I looked in the windows and took some pictures, but unfortunately this was the phone that went crazy and ruined my memory card. Let it be some consolation that the inside of the dredge wasn't much to look at. It was basically a bunch of pulleys and cables. For some reason it reminded me of the inside of a feed mill.

I had gotten in touch with the Iditarod folks. They confirmed the sign was inside for retouch work but didn't say anything about Hillary supporters. When I asked if we could come and take pictures of it inside the garage, they said that wouldn't be a problem. We planned this for the following day, which was Friday. You'll have to check out my handiwork with photoshop. The picture on the cover of us under the sign was taken inside the shop, with a dump truck in the background. Using photoshop I made us taller, and replaced the dump truck with the city square of Nome. It just occurred to me I could go through each picture in the book and make myself look slim and trim. Maybe you should be suspicious if I look very thin and muscular in the next book! I might as well give myself a big Alaskan beard too.

Above: There are quite a few children in Teller. Below: The generator building.

Above: A boat in "dry dock" on the beach. Boats like these are valuable in a community surrounded by water. Below: Salmon drying in the sun.

On Friday we wandered around the town of Nome doing some more sight seeing. We went to a museum, which we discovered was closed for renovations. It was in the same building as the library. After that we went to the square of Nome (also called Anvil City Square) and took some family pictures in front of the giant gold pan. We also took pictures in front of old St. Joseph's Church. The church was originally built in 1901 and served as a church until 1944. In 1995 it was donated to the city of Nome and moved to the square and restored. It is now a community building. The church used to have a light in the steeple that would guide incoming mushers. It is one of the most visible buildings in the city, especially from the air.

In an ironic twist of fate, our clothing colors matched the colors of the church. The one family photo is on the back of Marlene's cookbook, and we have had many people ask if we intentionally coordinated the colors. While we would love to claim credit for such coordination, the answer is no, it was completely by chance. For some reason I wore my hiking shoes, and Marlene shudders every time she sees the photo (I'm not really a slave to fashion).

Later we found the Iditarod sign and took pictures with it. Because it was inside the Nome maintenance shed, it was a bit tricky getting decent photos. Missie had a wide angle lens on her camera, and she was able to just so get the whole sign in the photo. I touched the sign, and it was indeed tacky from drying sealer or lacquer. This is yet another cool thing about the Iditarod and Alaska. I doubt you could go down to the Daytona speedway and be welcomed with open arms by race officials to wander around the track.

You can only look at a sign so long, and eventually we went back to our motel, but not before dropping a sack of money at a local restaurant. Even Subway is expensive. With trying to cut corners our family's bill was around $80.

I wanted to go gold panning, but was afraid to just go try anywhere. Along the one road we had stopped and panned in a creek but didn't find anything. Also worrisome was the potential of jumping someone's claim, and then having them jump you. After some research, I found a place where you could pay to prospect. Now I'm a little leery of gold panning tourist traps. These are fine, but there is something a little cheesy about going to pan out dirt that the tourist trap threw gold in before you arrived. First, you know that they are not going to throw large nuggets in. Second, it feels a little like hunting pigs in the barnyard. While I wouldn't tell someone that it is wrong, it would certainly not feel like you were accomplishing anything worthwhile. Why even bother going to Alaska if you prospect this way, just buy some

Above: I hadn't really imagined we would take this picture in a garage, with a dump truck in the background, but I'm glad we could at least get a picture with the famous sign! Below: Anvil City Square, with the world's largest gold pan! Those are dredge buckets in front of it.

Above: The "Three Lucky Swedes" with the old St. Joseph Catholic Church in the background. Below: Our family in front of the church door. We were actually very cold when the picture was taken.

gold flakes, throw it in your flowerbed, and pan it out.

Now, I realize that maybe not everyone always thinks like I do 100% of the time. Somewhat recently I was approached by a retired lady named Lois Graybill. We have known Lois for a long time. She leaned towards me like she was sharing a secret, and whispered "I need professional counseling." I was a bit taken aback, as Lois always seemed stable and level-headed. Then she reminded me of the caption in another book that says something to the effect, "If the thought of panning for gold in the Alaskan wilderness doesn't make your heart beat faster you need professional counseling." So, if you prefer panning gold at a tourist trap, or even prefer not panning at all, that is totally fine.

While researching I came across a place called Akau Gold. This didn't seem like a typical tourist trap. I called the number and reached a lady in California. She said we were welcome to stop in at the camp on Saturday (which was the next day), and have a try at panning, and that she would let them know we were stopping. She also assured me it would be an authentic experience. She described it as at "Mile 3" down Glacier Creek Road. Like many places in Alaska, it didn't have an official street address. Because we didn't have anything else to do that afternoon (Friday) we decided to drive down Glacier Creek Road and see if we could find the place. It was only a few miles outside of Nome.

Glacier Creek Road turned out to be very washed out and full of ruts. One spot I had to gun the van to get momentum to plough through a ditch. We didn't find the place, and ended up coming back to Nome again. After studying their website more carefully, I remembered seeing a sign shown on their site, so I was confident we could find it the next day. By the looks of the sign, it was not going to be a disappointment.

Bottom: Sign at the end of the lane. Is the crutch a warning to potential claim jumpers?
Right: Second sign at the end of the lane.

Gold Strike
Chapter 22

Shane and I were excited to pan for gold in a place that actually might have some. I almost didn't take Shane along, as it was $150 a head to pan. But we don't get to Nome very often, and the next time might be in the dead of winter, so I figured he might as well come along. Marlene and the rest were going to drop us off and come back four hours later, as they wanted to go look around town.

Pulling into the gold camp, or as it is officially called "Alaska Gold & Resort," we didn't see anyone. I started to wonder if maybe we did go to the wrong place, when I noticed a fellow in a beat up old Ford pickup, piled high with scrap metal. He introduced himself as "Augie" ("just remember it rhymes with doggie," he said) and confirmed we were at the right place. "Good thing you caught me," he said, "I was just running to town with a load of scrap." I could tell we had indeed left the tourist traps far behind in the rear view mirror.

"Let's go find Bob," Augie said, and motioned for us to drive after him. We drove up another lane for about a quarter mile and came to what looked like a bunk house. After some time a fellow named Bob came out and introduced himself. Augie, Bob, Shane, and myself headed down to where the sluice boxes were set up. At this I mentioned to Augie we had purchased the panning package, as the sluice package was quite a bit more. "Oh well," he said, "Let's just use the sluice." They were between groups, and the sluices were open. Later, I was very glad we got the chance to use the sluice. If you plan a trip, just pay extra right away to make sure to get a sluice box to use.

Augie left for town, leaving Bob there with us. Bob gave us a quick run down of how everything worked, which we were already familiar with, but it was nice to get pointers from someone who actually knew what they were doing. I asked Bob where the dirt came from that we were working, and he pointed to the nearby Anvil creek. "We take the pay loader down there, scoop it up, and dump it here," he explained. That satisfied my concern that the experience wasn't authentic. And what a history lesson, panning dirt from the same creek that triggered the last great gold rush in the United States!

After the sluice was running, Bob announced we had it under control, and he was heading back up to the bunkhouse, lodge, or whatever it was. Before leaving he pointed to a part of the dirt pile. "Here is where you'll find your pay dirt," he said. Later Augie said the same thing, but pointed to a

bove: Bob explains to Shane and myself how to do something, probably gold panning, or perhaps Sasquatch tracking. Below: The sluice where we shoveled the dirt into.

Above: Panning gold is a great father/son activity! Below: Augie shows how to "clean up" the gold pan.

different part of the dirt pile! We decided to hedge our bets and shoveled from both spots.

So we shoveled, shoveled, and shoveled some more! Gold prospecting is not always as glamorous as people make it sound. But then again, neither is deer hunting. After we shoveled dirt for about an hour, Bob came by and showed us how to "clean up." This involved cleaning the sluice mat in a Rubbermaid tote and dumping the contents through a screen. After doing that, we panned it out. And we did find gold! Panning gold is much easier when there is actually gold in the pan. Being approximately 17 times heavier than dirt, gold sticks to the bottom of the pan almost like a magnet. After months of staring sideways at clumps of funny looking rocks, wondering if it was gold, we finally had the real thing. The final step was taking a "sniffer" and sucking the gold up out of the pan and depositing it into a glass vial.

Finding actual gold got Shane and myself hungry for more. Bob said we could go ahead and do it all over again, so we fired up the sluice and started shoveling. After about another hour or two we shut down the water pump and "cleaned up". I think we got a total of about $100 worth of gold. So don't sell the farm and leave tomorrow for Nome. However it was a very fun, interesting experience and I recommend it to everyone.

Bob had a humorous story about Augie and his son. Over the winter Augie and his family live down in California. I suppose this helps them fully realize and appreciate the freedom of Alaska. After school started in the fall, the teacher had all the students share what they did that summer. Augie's son

(unfortunately I don't know his name) said that he had been to Alaska and mined gold all summer. The teacher thought this was a fantastic story and scolded him for lying. She then called Augie to report this misbehavior, only to find out that his son was telling the truth!

I asked Bob if anyone ever found enough gold to pay the actual prospecting fees (you can keep all the gold you found). He said it happens quite often. Several years back three guys found $50,000 worth of gold with a metal detector in one afternoon. That made the newspapers! And I'm sure kept customers coming for a long time afterward.

Above: A commercial mining operation just outside of Nome. Below: Shane, Augie, and Matt pose for the camera. Matt is holding the gold recovered.

Above: Looking down the coast line from about 250 feet in the air. You can see the entrance of the small boat harbor sticking out. Below: The small boat harbor. This is all artificial, in 1900 there was no harbor here! This resulted in all cargo being hauled ashore in small boats.

Above: The Nome Nugget Inn. Below: A birds eye view over Nome taken from the plane as we came in to land. You can see old St. Joseph's Church in the center.

bove: Modern day gold prospecting. Prospectors use suction to pull material from the sea floor
) into a sluice type apparatus to collect gold. Below: Old St. Joseph's Catholic Church, where
e took family pictures. A light used to be kept in the steeple to guide mushers into Nome.

The sad day when we had to leave Nome arrived. It was just as well, with the price of food and gas, we wouldn't have lasted much longer. I dropped everyone (except Shane) off at the airport, and headed back to the motel to return the van. The airport was only about two miles from the motel, so we just walked to the airport. Walking to the airport, we met Augie driving the other way, and he waved going past.

Arriving at the airport, we discovered Bob there. He was flying out on the same flight to Anchorage. This time I was extremely careful not to have any bullets in my carry on. I did bring a shovel along that I had purchased in Nome. They made me tape some cardboard around the bottom of the metal edge. I never did see the shovel again. Oh well, if the airline is going to lose my luggage, it might as well be the cheap little shovel.

I did bring some sand along from the beach in Nome. Locals would probably find this hilarious, but after paying so much for food and gas about the only souvenir I could afford was a coffee can full of sand. With a little airport like Nome, I figured it would be easy peasy to fly through security and get on the plane. This turned out to not be the case.

First, Shane tried to go through security with his favorite pocket knife. Sorry! It was hand over the knife to the TSA agent, or stay in Nome. As he was half in tears, my infamous Makita camera bag went through the scanner. Once again there was a buzz of excitement. "What is this?" the attendant asked, pulling out my coffee can. I explained that I had gotten sand from the beach to bring back, all the while hoping I hadn't unknowingly committed a felony. "We'll have to test it in our lab;" the lady announced. She went into a back room and took some of the sand out and did who knows what with it.

Our next bag went through security, and this also caused some excitement. I wondered what in the world could be the problem now. The agent pulled out the children's playdough, which we had purchased in Nome. As it turns out, playdough and C4 plastic explosives look identical. I assured the agents I wouldn't let my children play with C4, but the playdough was taken to the lab for analyzation. Naturally, all the while Mary Kate was throwing fits about something. After a few minutes the tests came through "all clear", and we were allowed to board the plane with our sand and playdough. By now Bob probably thought he had helped some terrorists go gold panning.

The flight back to Anchorage was fairly uneventful, except for some

some rather rough turbulence. Mary Kate seemed to think we were doomed, but we made it to Anchorage.

At Anchorage we picked up our motor home at the Airport Parking lot, paid our rather hefty parking bill, and headed south. For some unexplainable reason, Missie chose to stay in Alaska an additional week or two. The next book may shed more light on this subject.

So we hit the road, and headed back to the lower 48 for a quick road trip in the RV. After taking care of business, we cruised back to Alaska in plenty of time for moose season (is this a record or what– over 8,000 miles of driving covered in a single paragraph). We really do need to look into flying more!

Below: This sign is from a Virginia rest area! Do they really have trouble with people unloading livestock at rest areas?

Below: I love Canada's Road Signs!

I always figured automatic car washes were a money scam and didn't do a good job. However, I decided to give one a try. I was very impressed with the results! The children loved it too, except for Mary Kate, who was terrified. Above: Before. Below: After!

Marlene Threatens to Burn Down the Cabin
Chapter 24

Marlene is typically a very reserved person and puts up with a lot. The one day she said, "I would love to burn the cabin down." I chuckled at this joke, and said something like, "I hope you're joking." She smiled back sweetly and said, "I'm not joking." Whoa. To be sure, there are occasional, minor inconveniences with our small, off-the-grid cabin. For example, if you forget to turn the iron off, and it is on all night, it runs the cabin's batteries dead. This makes me grumpy, and requires me to run the generator if the sun is not out. The shower also is still a bit unpredictable; and then there is the weekly ritual of trying to find out why the pipes (including drains) froze up.

One day, back in the late spring or early summer, Marlene had found a few acres for sale closer to Soldotna. I usually figure moving closer to town is acting a bit like Lot, posting his tent closer to Sodom. I'm not sure if Lot's wife ever threatened to burn his tent down, but I think Soldotna is quite a bit better than Sodom was. Faced with the prospect of leaving Alaska for good, or moving a bit closer to town, I elected for the latter. I must admit to becoming soft myself, as the prospect of electric service appealed to me greatly.

Finally, in September sometime, our house construction began. Alaska requires no permits, so we could simply just start digging. While it is not required, I elected to have a DEC approved septic system. This means if I ever wanted to sell the place, or get a home equity loan, it would be much easier. While I loathe both of those ideas, it doesn't hurt sometimes to plan ahead so more options are available.

I decided construction should start in the spring of 2017. But when I talked to my excavator, Dan Zimmerman, he thought I should do it right away. We have a fairly long lane leading into the new house location, and it goes right over some muskeg. Dan explained in the spring, when the ground was soft, the heavy equipment was likely to tear up this roadway, which I share with the neighbor. I doubted the neighbor would be too happy with me destroying the lane.

Like all the land I seem to buy in Alaska, this land has a lot of muskeg (swamp). Alan dug a test hole for me, and we were all relieved to find good dirt underneath. Had the test hole filled right up with water, it would have been a sign of bad things to come. Since our property also contains mineral rights (unusual for land sold in Alaska), I was hoping to see gold nuggets in the test hole. But sadly that didn't happen. Wouldn't it be great to find enough gold to pay off the property?

I gave Dan the go ahead to start working, and he went right at it. He installed the septic, put in a driveway, and lined up Marvin Schrock to do the concrete work.

After the concrete work the sub floor was installed, and then it was all covered with plastic. The framing will start in the spring of 2017, provided I don't go bankrupt before then. Construction in Alaska is a good deal more expensive than I figured, especially if it is "done right". I should have just put the house on pier blocks!

Later I met with the house designer, Ervin Beachy. He explained that most of his clients came to him before they built the foundation and basement. That would have been nice, but as I told him they were in a hurry to get it in while the weather was nice. Despite these limitations he drew up a plan that I thought was very acceptable.

We decided to order the kitchen from Ethan Zimmerman. His shop is located in Kenton, Delaware. Our family visited their facility in the spring while at a book signing nearby, and we were impressed with the quality of his shop's work. You know it was good if we are willing to drag the kitchen 4,000 miles.

The house basement will also be used as the meeting point for the new church in Alaska. Several families, Andy and Tabitha Stoltzfus, Dwight and Kristen Wenger, and ourselves have committed to the project. We are planning to be affiliated with BMA (Biblical Mennonite Alliance). Pray for this new work. We did not settle on a church name for sure yet, but it will probably be called "River of Life Fellowship".

These pictures on the previous page and on this page are of the basement and driveway construction. Marvin Schrock's crew is doing the concrete work.

The Berry Pickers Exposed
Chapter 25

I have been accused of constantly trying to sell everyone something, all the time. It apparently is some sort of reflex I have. For example, when I bought the Mallard, the guy selling it (a complete stranger), accused me of trying to talk him into moving to Alaska. One time when I was five years old I received a weaving set to make little potholders. I whipped up a batch and took them along to kindergarten and sold them for 25 cents apiece. Not only did I sell out, I took orders for more. If only I had accepted credit cards, I may have been able to command a higher price. Maybe not, as I don't know many kindergartners who carry Visa and MasterCard. I should have also had a website, but in 1987 the Internet didn't exist (well maybe in government labs but not as it is today).

One of my friends, someone who I would have not expected (but wishes to remain anonymous, we'll call him Lee), asked me to send him links to land for sale in Alaska. I obliged, and sent him several advertisements for 9 or 10 acre parcels. His reply was that these were "not big enough." After searching some more, I found a 40 acre lot outside of Soldotna. He thought that was getting better, but still not what he had in mind. Finally I found an 80 acre lot. This he found more interesting but still wanted something larger. He wanted to build vacation rental cabins, and it wouldn't do to have them crowded together in a heap.

This went back and forth a bit, over a week or two of time. During that time Paul Weaver (the same Paul from Book 3) emailed me with a listing. It was 248 acres of pure Alaska. And it was right down the street from my land! I figured if this wasn't enough for Lee, then nothing would be. So I sent the information over to Lee, half wondering if maybe this chunk of land was too big. Nope, it wasn't too big. Within a week or two Lee had put money down on it, and it was under contract. Suddenly I felt a bit nervous. Had Lee put all this money on the line because of something I said? Now that is a little bit scary, but Lee assured me he wouldn't hold anything against me in the off chance it didn't work out. It is hard to imagine owning too much of a good thing, so I'm sure it will be fine.

In an ironic twist of fate, I discovered the people selling the land were allegedly the infamous "Berry Pickers" of Book 2. This information was divulged by another neighbor, who wishes to remain anonymous. Apparently in a conversation with the anonymous neighbor, they made the comment

Above: The cabin looks better from a distance, but we'll get that taken care of before you come rent it. A free bulldozer came with the property! Below: The Alaska Acres cabin up close.

Hopefully nobody minds, but the "Berry Picker" psychedelic paint scheme is going to get torn out and burned. We will replace it with more traditional rustic Alaskan décor!

that they had helped themselves to our cabin while we were away. Thankfully they weren't thieves, leaving quite a bit of ammunition alone, along with some other valuables such as deep cycle batteries. What they had done was make a mess in the sink cooking up some of my instant noodles. Then they left a note explaining they had gotten lost berry picking, and as a result sought refuge in our cabin. This would have been completely permissible in an emergency, however this happened in the summer time, not to mention they were within half a mile of their own cabin! I didn't bother approaching them about it, as they could have done much worse. I had no solid proof, and they were leaving the neighborhood anyway.

This particular neighborhood had actually gotten the local nickname "felony acres." It seems the lure of cheap land, no zoning, and off-the-grid living appealed to more folks than just myself. Locals did assure me that it has been cleaned up quite a bit in recent years. And besides, I would much rather live here than say, Chicago. If I had to choose between felons as neighbors or zoning, I'll take felons. In Chicago you have both.

After this land deal was lined up, it was time to build some cabins. Since Lee did not live in Alaska, he wanted me to get things going. Now I have built a cabin, and with all modesty, I must mention a few tree houses. Sadly a realtor once blamed one of my tree houses for my property not selling. It just shows that every industry has shady characters. However some of my friends, cousins, relatives, etc. were chomping at the bit to come up to Alaska. It only made sense that they should come and do all the work.

One of the first relatives to bite was my cousin, Adam Sensenig. This is the same Adam that used to live in Mexico. He helped out at an orphanage, where we drove to in the $400 van pulling the trailer load of food. You can read about that in Marlene's cookbook. Adam agreed to fly up and bring his wife, Suni, along. Josh also relented and agreed to fly up, but oddly his wife Janice didn't want to come along. Adam now works in construction, so he really knows how to build things. Josh, on the other hand, spends all his time making new beard balm recipes in his kitchen. He then sells the balm online and wholesales to stores. But Josh did help me build my cabin/house, and that is still standing, even taking a 7.1 magnitude earthquake without fail.

One small detail that I overlooked with my meticulous planning was my cow moose tag and the opening season date. The regular moose season I had not bothered going hunting, because I pulled the cow moose tag earlier in February. In our area a legal bull has to have a 50 inch rack. The instant I say this, everybody's response is, "How do you get the bull to stand still while you measure the rack?" Or a similar reply. Well, the truth is, you can't tell. Sure everyone has their special formulas, like "Look at the ears, draw a line through them, pretend another ear is here or there, etc, etc," and then you're good. Spike bulls are also legal, but are almost as rare as 50 inch racks. The penalties for shooting a non legal bull are pretty stiff. Being confident, I decided to just skip bull moose season and go for what was almost a guaranteed hunt, a cow moose. When I realized that Adam and Josh would be showing up shortly after cow moose season started, I wasn't fazed. "I'll just have to shoot one before they get here," I told Marlene.

I did not take the moose picture below; it is from Wikipedia. This demonstrates the requirements for a legal moose in many parts of Alaska. Regulations do vary across the state. I believe this particular moose has a rack well over 50 inches.

This picture is under public domain. Photographer Donna Dewhurst. Obtained from Wikipedia. This actual picture is not under copyright, so use it all you want.

Cow Moose Season
Chapter 26

When I drew my cow moose tag, I was very excited. The drawings are held in February and are posted online. Many hunts are drawing only. As soon as I saw the good news, I called my neighbor, Richard (the same Richard that almost sank with the *El Dan* in Alaska Sea Escapes). He gave me a hearty congratulations and assured me that my chances of getting a cow moose could be scientifically calculated at 125%. Richard has taken over 20 moose in his lifetime, so he knows a thing or two about moose hunting. We both had a good laugh over the idea of me not finding a cow moose to shoot.

As time passed, I discussed this practically guaranteed hunt with my dad. He always wanted to see someone shoot a moose, so he agreed to come up and go along. A bit suspicious that there is a brown bear behind every bush, he informed me he was bringing his .300 Winchester Magnum along. I booked some tickets for him, and the trip was set.

We picked him up at the Anchorage Ted Stevens airport a day or two before the opening of cow moose season. I assumed he wanted to go hunting too, bringing his gun and all. Black bear season is open year round, and non-residents can buy a black bear tag for $250. However, when he purchased his license he got a $20 license for hunting spruce grouse! I told him even in Alaska we don't hunt spruce grouse (or chickens as we call them) with a .300 Winchester Magnum!

A few days before cow moose season I discovered a snag in my well laid plans. The area my tag was good for did not extend to my property! My only choice was to hunt much closer to Homer than I wanted. When Richard heard this, he said, "It wouldn't be a problem, we can hunt at his parents' place." But then we discovered they weren't in the tag area either! Suddenly the scientifically determined success rate of 125% was dropping like a rock. Finally the first day of cow moose season came, dawning clear and cold.

This was my first time actually hunting in the winter (late October, which maybe isn't winter but really close), as before it was always spring, summer or fall when I hunted. I had prepared ahead of time by ordering Arctic Pro Muck Boots (good for -60 degrees Fahrenheit) insulated coveralls, long johns, and many layers of clothes. I didn't want to freeze to death!

Shane, Dad, Richard, and myself took our van down to Homer. But first we swung by the Alaska State Police barracks in Anchor Point. There we told the officer that we were heading to "shoot a cow moose" and if

Above: Shane and Richard look for moose tracks. Below: This is the ridge I hunted quite a bit for cow moose.

anybody calls in about a cow moose shot "it was us." It is a pretty rare thing to be able to legally shoot a cow moose, so we figured that people would be calling us in left and right. This turned out to be the least of our problems.

Not being a seasoned moose hunter, I made a mistake in my hunting preparations. When I hunt deer in Pennsylvania I usually go out in the woods and sit still. Occasionally (very occasionally) a deer will actually walk by, and I will shoot it. This is not how Richard hunted. After we found a piece of public hunting land in the tag area, we decided to hike around on it. And hike we did! Up ravines, through streams and gulleys, and back again. My heavily insulated Arctic Pro boots felt like blocks of concrete on my feet, and I huffed and puffed like a steam engine, with beads of sweat all over my fore-head. Shane danced around like it was nothing, and my dad seemed only slightly worse off than myself.

Around 11 A.M. Richard announced it was a waste of time to look any further, as the moose don't move around any more until the evening. So we headed back to the van, which had the trailer hooked up with the four wheeler on it (for dragging the moose out). Upon returning home, I discovered my cell phone was missing! It was fairly new, and I certainly didn't want to lose it.

That afternoon I went back out to the same area where we were that morning to look for my cell phone. To my shock, we found it laying in the grass near the road. Chalk that one up as a first! As I was marveling over finding the phone, a pickup truck pulled up. "Hey, what are you doing on private land!" the driver barked. I was puzzled, as I had checked the map, and I was pretty certain this was state owned public land. When I inquired where the line was, he snorted and drove off. Later I checked the line with a GPS and discovered the property line went through the middle of his front yard and he had old dilapidated vehicles parked on state land! That might explain why he didn't want to point out the property line.

The next day, full of enthusiasm, we headed out yet again, going back to the same spot. But, it was the same sad case. We did find a bunch of large brown bear foot prints, which were fascinating to look at. I did have a valid brown bear tag, so I would have been quite happy had it shown up. It wasn't that there were no moose signs, because moose tracks were everywhere. But we didn't see a single moose!

Soon the initial vigor that we had approached the guaranteed moose hunt with, started to wane. Saturday, instead of going moose hunting with me, Dad and Shane went out and hunted spruce grouse. Shane shot two with our 12 gauge, and Dad showed him how to butcher them.

Above: Dad and Shane with the spruce grouse, or "chicken" as we call them. Below: Left to Right-Dad, Josh, Adam and Suni. Shane's spruce grouse is in one of the pans on the table.

Adam, Suni, and Josh showed up that weekend, complicating the moose hunting; but we were glad to have them anyway. Adam and Suni slept in the motorhome, and Josh and Dad on our couches. This arrangement was snug, but it worked.

Alan Reinford had graciously allowed us to borrow his Chevy pickup (I know, I really need to buy my own truck), and on Monday, Josh and Adam took it down to Spenard's Building Supply in Homer. While they were fetching lumber, I again crept stealthily around the woods down in the Homer area. Again, I saw nothing alive. I might as well have gone hunting on the moon.

Meanwhile, Adam and Josh were really making things happen down at "Alaska Acres" as we decided to call the 248 acres. They framed up the floor, which was set on pier blocks, like my house. Even Richard seemed to write off my moose hunting abilities, and started helping in the cabin construction! The trusses for the cabin were sourced from the old bath house we had torn down the year before. In hindsight it would have been cheaper to order brand new trusses. But who would have known tearing down a 36-year-old free building wouldn't be a good idea? Life is just full of the unexpected.

Above: Adam and Josh set trusses. Below: "Alaska Acres" from the air by drone. My property is ahead and to the right a bit, about half a mile away.

At the beginning of the book, Josh talks a little bit about this adventure. But he exaggerated a few points, and neglected some details, making yours truly look a bit like a raving lunatic. I'll attempt to avoid being redundant, so here it goes.

Naturally, it is almost a crime to visit Alaska and not go halibut fishing. Josh had never actually gone out in a boat halibut fishing, despite being in Alaska four or five times. Adam and Suni had never even been to Alaska before, so it was high time to get these people out in a boat. In family devotions Samantha had taken up praying that she would "get to go fishing in Daddy's boat." So all these people, plus Shane, got to go along fishing. It is true we had some minor setbacks with the big boat. Somehow water had weaseled it's way into my waterproof boat ignition. This causes the ignition to not turn, so we needed to thaw it out. I don't remember how we did it, but I don't think it was with a blow torch.

What Josh says is true; to have a reliable boating experience you should have at least four boats. Being a math whiz and all, I arrived at this conclusion using some complex, time tested formulas. But no sense boring readers with algebra, I'll get on with the story. We decided to take the 27 foot boat, which is currently named *Doesn't Leak*. Josh's bunny trail on my articulate use of the English language, the Third Reich, and theology, involving this particular boat may have been because of some additional boat name suggestions I had made while cheerfully working through the issues with it.

After we started the boat, we determined an issue with the out drive hydraulics. When we pushed the down button, the hydraulic motor would just click. We hauled the boat down to the dock anyway, and replicated the experiment with the same results, clearly demonstrating the hydraulics did not work. Josh also mentioned some issues with trailer lights. Actually it's hard for me to recall ever even having trailers with working lights, so perhaps he is accurate in that portrayal. It's not that I don't like having trailer lights, it's just that they are so temporary. To keep them working all the time I would need to have a mechanic follow me around with a parts truck.

Every person has some sort of talent, some more than others. One of my talents is I have the ability to take a new trailer, and merely by thinking of the highway patrol, cause all the lights to stop working. This phenomenon occurred many times, with new and old trailers. Unfortunately this ability does not extend into useful areas of life.

The boat hydraulics were only a minor problem, as we had a spare boat, the 18' aluminum Lund. Now this was not the first time we used it, as obviously I talked about fishing in it with Henry. We had taken it out quite a few times by this point. I felt pretty confident it would work. My dad also came along down to the dock, however he refused to get into the boat. Apparently he has some sort of salt water phobia, or maybe a fear of seagulls. For whatever reason, he refused the chance for a relaxing boat ride.

After launching the boat, it performed flawlessly. We cruised up the coastline to Anchor Point, where I hear the big halibut hang out. Josh was the only one who did not have a fishing license, so he had to help Samantha fish. Naturally, they caught the only halibut, a small one only weighing about 15 pounds.

The wind started picking up, and the temperature was hovering around 35 degrees. The tide was coming in, and we lost our anchor. At this we decided to just head back, as everyone was starting to get chilled. I fired up the engine, and then the squealing started from the boat alarm. I don't like hearing alarms, especially when I'm out on a boat. A quick check over the engine, fuel and oil tank revealed that we were out of oil! This was puzzling, as the oil tank had been half full when we gassed up. The oil tank typically lasts for many tanks of gas. Some more poking and prodding revealed all the oil was in the bottom of the boat! Additional research revealed an oil line had broken, and instead of pumping the oil into the motor it pumped it into the bottom of the boat. Being the frugal type, I certainly didn't want to ruin the engine by running it without oil.

While all this was going on Adam called my dad and informed him that we were "dead in the water." That term always sounds bad, no matter how optimistically you say it. After a short conversation Adam told my dad he had to get back to helping us attempt to fix the boat. To save his phone battery, Adam then turned his phone off. Sometime in the near future I will add an auxiliary 12 volt power hookup for phone chargers.

First we tried to splice the oil line back together. This clearly did not work. We had limited tools (a pocket knife and a screw driver), and the boat rocking on the increasingly rough waves did not help.

The outboard has a big heavy cover over it. With Adam and Josh's help, I picked the cover off and set it down in the boat. To my relief there was an internal oil reservoir on the engine. Later I also realized we could have dumped some oil straight into the gas tank, had this reservoir been empty (we had a spare quart of 2 stroke oil onboard). Sometimes it is hard to think straight in emergencies.

Right: The Mercury outboard without the engine cover.

Right: The broken oil tank cap that caused trouble. A second line is supposed to attach where the hole is located.

Below: The emergency reservoir that held enough oil to get back to Homer.

Now that we were sure the engine wouldn't burn up on us, we fired it up and headed back towards Homer. I drove slowly to conserve fuel, as I didn't know how long the emergency oil reservoir would last. It would also be terribly hard to see where we were going. This was the first time I used the Lund at night, and I realized that the lights needed some extra work. There is a bar across the center of the boat, with a light bar mounted on it. This light bar is indeed very bright, but because it is in the middle of the boat it has the effect of lighting up the front of the boat, making it even harder to see through the darkness ahead of the boat. I also realized the importance of having a GPS. The boat does have a GPS, a nice little Hummingbird unit. Without the GPS we would have had no idea where we were going, as we were too far from Homer to see its lights.

As we slowly puttered back towards Homer, someone mentioned we should call my dad and let him know we weren't dead. Adam turned his phone back on and called him, and got a rather animated response. My dad, not being able to get ahold of Adam on his phone (because it was turned off) assumed we were all approaching death's doorstep, floating in the inlet, fighting the onset of hypothermia. I did not have my phone along; it was with Marlene. To complicate matters, my dad had discovered our satellite powered emergency signaling device lying in the van. This further strength-ened his theory that we were in desperate straights, on the brink of death, helpless to summon help.

Due to his concern, he called the Coast Guard, who was in the pro-cess of locating their nearest cutter to our assumed position. They were also discussing dispatching a chopper. I like helicopter rides and all, but this was one ride I wasn't ready to take. It would have been a real shock to have a chopper come hover over us and throw down a rope. Not only that, those things cost like $18,000 an hour to run. Who pays that bill? I sure didn't want to. I quickly assured dad we were just fine, we'll be back soon, and call off the Coast Guard! He did let me know, in no uncertain terms, what he thought about me leaving the GPS communication signaler lying in the van. But what am I to say? Maybe he would have needed help on the dock, and could have used that to summon help (if that battery wasn't dead).

What everyone seemed to forget in all this panic (I had not forgotten) was the fact we had an extra engine in the boat! Yes, mounted on the back, right beside the 150 HP outboard, was a humble little 8 HP "kicker" motor. It would have taken all night to get back to Homer with this little motor, and I'm not sure if it would have been big enough to power us against the tide. However, it would have been large enough to get us the two miles in to shore. From there we would have tied up the boat, had someone bring us tools or whatever we needed in a car, repaired the boat, and continued to Homer. But it would have caused delay and been inconvenient.

Finally, after all this fanfare, we slowly cruised into Homer's small boat harbor. As I tied the boat to the dock, I realized the fuel gauge was flat on E. The real potential crisis for that evening was running out of fuel. Out in the rough water I had not realized this, because the bouncing of the boat makes the fuel gauge needle fly around wildly. As I thought over why we used so much more fuel than normal, I realized that when we went out, we were going against the tide. While we fished the tide turned, and we fought it again on the way back in. The tides in Cook Inlet are very high, as much as 30 feet at times, so this is a serious current to work against. This made the engine work harder and burned more fuel than normal. I think I did have a spare two gallon gas can in the boat, but you can burn up two gallons very quickly. For example, my 27 foot boat has a 100 gallon gas tank. Remember: Nothing about boating is cheap!

On the way back we stopped at an oasis of refreshment: McDonalds. Not much stimulates your appetite like being out in the freezing cold for several hours. A tip for folks waiting for their loved ones to return to the dock: Read *Alaska Sea Escapes* to pass the time.

Enjoying quality Mexican food at Don Jose's in Homer. I always thought "selfie sticks" were for proud, arrogant folks, but when Adam pulled one out I decided maybe they had a place in society.

More Cabin Construction
Chapter 28

Adam and Josh still had work to do on the cabin. I still went out moose hunting every day, but by now nobody even went along. Adam, Josh, and Richard really made things happen with the cabin. I was impressed how fast they framed it up. They were determined to have it "dried in" before they left. My determination was to shoot a moose before they left! I told Marlene I would be like "moss on a rock" in the woods. Silent, stealthy and deadly. She carefully concealed her awe with gales of laughter, suggesting instead I just spent the whole day on my phone looking at gun parts, and not even seeing the moose that were there.

Lee (the Alaska Acres investor) told me to take everyone out for a meal as part of their reward for coming up to help build cabins. He had given me this nifty credit card to swipe that was connected with his account. So one evening I took everyone to Don Jose's in Homer. We had a good time and Suni (Adam's wife) gave it a stamp of approval. If anyone knows what good Mexican food should taste like, it would be Suni. Then came the sad time for Josh, Dad, Adam, and Suni to fly back to Pennsylvania. Dad was the first to fly out, leaving Saturday evening. The rest went Sunday evening or Monday, I don't remember which anymore.

The sad conclusion: Cow moose season ended without me getting a moose! However, the draw permits are coming around again soon. Maybe I'll pull a permit for somewhere else this time. I put in for the antlerless moose drawing near the place above Fairbanks where we gold panned. No, I never saw any moose there, but I figured maybe we'll try "reverse psychology." The moose probably all go hide there in moose season.

Above: Josh and Adam frame up the front porch, and are ready for windows. Below: The cabin is all "dried in." And yes, that is Ol' Blue in those pictures! Still running strong!

Bears!
Chapter 29

When we first set up our tent in Alaska a few years ago, I was very concerned about bears. After not seeing any bears for years, I began to think they didn't even exist in that area. One day I talked to a neighbor that claimed he had gotten mauled where our house is (years before we or the house were there). He seemed like an honest enough fellow, but I was a tiny bit dubious. As a security precaution I put up some game cameras on the field lane and our regular lane going into our property. Over the past year or two we have gotten pictures of wolves, coyotes, moose and many birds.

My neighbor Richard helps me keep tabs on the cameras, and I told him to check them whenever he wants. Since he just lives down the road, whatever wildlife he sees is likely to go through his property sometime. One day Richard called me. "Hey, we got some bear pictures!" he exclaimed. We were both excited about this. I didn't waste time checking for myself. Sure enough, there were quite a few brown bear pictures on the camera.

Then one day I discovered a bear had ripped the seat off of my snow-machine. This was parked pretty close to the cabin and was a bit unnerving. After Marlene saw the pictures, and my snowmobile, she suddenly gained a keen interest in firearms. We did get even more bear pictures, some as close as 300 feet from the cabin. Bears do keep to themselves. So far we have not seen any "in person." I'm hoping that it stays that way. Just maybe one will show up in bear season!

On an interesting, embarrassing side note, I have seen more bears at our place in PA than our place in Alaska. One evening, while in PA, I heard a noise on the front porch. I walked outside, only to discover a black bear (no grizzly's in Pa) standing about 20 feet away from me! I quickly retreated back into the cabin. The bear had torn up a 50 pound bag of dog food and dragged it off into the woods, where it proceeded to eat it. After I went back outside with my 12 gauge, I yelled at the bear until it finally left. When it did leave, the dog food bag was empty. I do enjoy watching bears, but preferably when they are not eating or ripping up my stuff.

I identified at least two different bears that used the lane in front of the game camera. I think these bears might both be the same one. The lighting is different in the two pictures which accounts for the coat colors being different.

Above: My Arctic Cat Snowmobile, or "Snowmachine" as we call them in Alaska. Note the big chunks missing from the foam. It also tore the seat cover off. Below: This bear wandered by. The pose isn't the most flattering in the world.

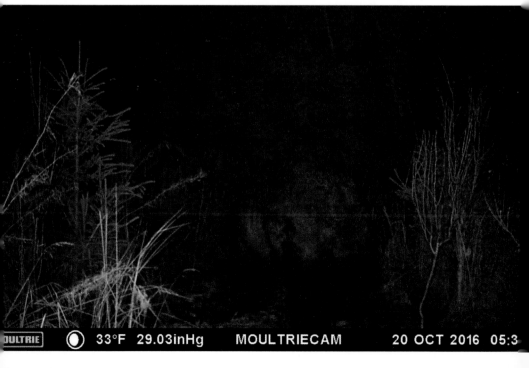

OULTRIE   33°F   29.03inHg   MOULTRIECAM   20 OCT 2016   05:3

I'm quite certain some folks will go into hysterics reading that I went alligator hunting, as though somehow this makes me less prone to like Alaska. Newsflash: Hardcore Alaskans don't wander around half frozen all the time; sometimes they take a break and thaw out. Recently I called Alan Reinford, and he was in Hawaii. We both agreed Hawaii was a nice place to visit but undoubtedly a horrible place to live. And yes, I have always wanted to shoot an alligator, and yes, I'm quite certain there are no alligators in Alaska, besides perhaps the zoo. And the zoo will not issue harvest permits. But there are no elephants or lions in Alaska either, and I wouldn't mind shooting one of each of those as well. But I digress.

Every year we do a few book signings to promote our books, meet our customers, etc. It was only logical that we would do one in Florida. A few months prior we talked to a few people and lined up a time and place. We decided to do it after the holidays, since we would once again be in Pennsylvania for those. From Pennsylvania it was only a short 18 hour drive to Sarasota, Florida. Naturally we decided to take advantages of Florida's natural resources, particularly their wild hogs. But, I had not given any thought to Florida's other more exotic creatures. With hogs in mind, I tossed some rifles in the car, and we headed south. I took my AR-15 along chambered in .50 caliber Beowulf, and also Shane's youth model .243 Winchester. These guns are fine hog killing machines, and both are legal to hunt with in Florida.

The last few times we were in Florida I tried unsuccessfully to catch the many little lizards that run around down there. I gave up because we kept finding snakes instead. It's a bit of a shock to chase a lizard into a bush, only to find a snake laying there. This time around I told Shane to take his BB gun along. I figured it would be fun to get in a little lizard hunting, since we weren't very good at catching them. Before our trip to Florida was over, the BB gun lay forgotten in the corner collecting dust. The hunt for reptiles got out of hand, and soon the BB gun wasn't nearly enough firepower.

After we planned the Florida trip, some of our in-laws also decided to get in on the action, and they also planned trips to Florida. It turned out we were able to share the house rent with Mike and Gina Kurtz. Gina is Marlene's sister.

One morning while both our families were eating at Der Dutchman, Mike and I were discussing this wild hog hunting foray. I certainly enjoy hog hunting, but I was pondering the possibilities of other hunts.

Someone, hopefully myself, but I'm not sure, came up with the brilliant idea to go alligator hunting. Perhaps it was because the backyard lizard hunting had proved poor. We both started checking out some guide websites, and before we knew what had happened we had a hunt booked for the very next day! To make matters even more interesting, Marlene wanted in on the action. As I said before, if Marlene approves, it's almost a guaranteed winner.

This exciting development was contingent on one thing: A babysitter. I called Marlene's parents, John and Mary, who were also down in Florida at the time. Thankfully it worked for Grandma to come over and babysit the next morning. This left me with an issue, though. Thinking we were going to be shooting large, tough skinned pigs, I only brought my .50 caliber. Shane did have his .243 Winchester (the gun is actually made by Remington) along so I decided to use that. The youth stock was shorter than what I was used to, but I had target practiced with his gun on numerous occasions.

We left around 7:00 A.M. the next morning, driving the limo. The alligator guide was down below Venus (not to be confused with Venice), which is almost a two hour drive from Sarasota. To hunt alligators on state land in Florida you need to pull a permit in a drawing, similar to Alaska's draw tag system. Your other option is to hunt on private land. This still requires a license, but the regulations are less strict, and anyone can just go buy a tag.

The GPS insisted we had arrived already when we actually had not. But using road signs and mailboxes, we were able to find the place. However, nobody was there! I was worried that maybe we had gone to the wrong place. Soon a fellow named Cliff did show up, and he was our guide for the morning. He had to make a quick run to town for some swamp buggy parts. Marlene's sister Gina also decided to come along, so it was Mike and Gina, Marlene and myself. Normally these hunts are done with an airboat, but they had not received rain for quite awhile and the water level was very low. We would need to just walk along the swamp bank. Hunting from an airboat does seem like more fun. In the future I would like to bring my bow along and shoot one like we do carp in Pennsylvania.

I wasn't sure what to expect with wild alligators. We have often seen alligators in zoos and Myakka State Park, but in those settings animals tend to be more laid back. People weren't always shooting at them or trying to stab them. Cliff said we needed to walk slowly and crouch down, or we would startle the gators and scare them off. All of us climbed into Cliff's truck, and we headed down to the swamp.

Above: Mike takes a shot at his gator, hitting it directly in the kill zone. Below: Mike with his gator.

The guide service charges by the size of the gator they find for you. Small gators are reasonably priced, but the larger they get the more expensive they are, over doubling in price after you get past 8 foot. This is because alligators grow slowly. A 13 foot alligator is over 60 years old. I'm also not trying to say the prices they command for a 60 year old alligator are not unreasonable, it's just that Marlene didn't want to give up having a kitchen in her new house for the sake of a 13 foot alligator. Even a 6 foot alligator is 8 years old or more. The folks with the private swamps don't want all the gators shot out of them, because it will take a very long time to grow more. So the price goes up as the size goes up. This is called "supply and demand."

Naturally liberal politicians would insist this system is unfair and caters to the rich, and that all prices should be the same, or better yet free. This would result in no alligators, or all the alligators being priced as 13 footers. All that to say, I'm not complaining about the pricing structure.

I wanted an 8 foot or less gator, and Mike said he would be content with a 4 to 6 footer. Cliff said he usually tried to get the larger gator first on a hunt, as the smaller ones were easier to find. Indeed, shortly after arriving at the swamp (one of several they hunt) we saw several small ones swimming around. My motto is "strike while the iron is hot", so I told Cliff I don't mind at all if Mike shoots one first. I knew how these things work, supposedly little ones are easy to find, but after we are looking for them, no more alligators.

Mike lined up to shoot a gator with his AR-15 chambered in 300 blackout. This nifty cartridge has similar ballistics as a 30-30 Winchester. Shooting gators is a little trickier than it sounds. You can get fairly close to them if you walk slow and stay down. They are not as jumpy as white tail deer, which will run if one of your stray nostril hairs blows in the wind. However, you need to hit the gator in the neck, right behind the eyeballs. If you miss this spot, you will wound the gator, but it will jump into the water and swim away. I'm not sure what Outwest Farm's policy is on this, but many places will charge you for that gator, because it will end up dying somewhere else in the swamp. They have one less gator, and you don't have any more gators. That is a bad deal for everyone!

One nice thing about gator hunting is that unless you startle them, you have about two hours to make the shot. The gators lay there like bumps on a log. Mike lined up for the shot, and pulled the trigger. A huge plume of dust flew up in front of him! There was a little bit of a knob between Mike and the gator, and while Mike's scope showed a clear shot, the path of the bullet was slightly lower, and impacted the dirt. This resulted in a clean miss.

which is the best kind. The first gator he was shooting at swam off, but to his right there was a second gator that hadn't moved through all this. This seems to indicate alligators are not very bright. Mike repositioned, and lined up for the second gator.

With Mike ready to shoot, I secretly wondered if his scope had been knocked off while traveling. I didn't realize what had actually transpired with his miss until afterward. As he squeezed off the shot, it became immediately apparent this wasn't a miss. A plume of water shot up right where the alligator was sitting, half submerged. The gator thrashed around furiously for a few seconds, then lay belly up in the water.

Because the gator was on the other side of a creek, Cliff used a huge treble hook on a large fish line to hook it and drag it over. After a few tries he hooked it and reeled it in. Mike had nailed the gator exactly at the kill spot, right behind the eyes. The 30 caliber bullet had done a nice clean job, and did not rip the gator to shreds like I had secretly suspected it might.

After the gator was on the bank Cliff hauled it about 50 yards from the bank. He explained even if you kill them cleanly, they will sometimes get up and walk off. They don't walk far, but if they are six feet from the creek bank they might make it to the creek and sink to the bottom, and you'll never find them again. Indeed, the rest of the day this critter would sporadically thrash around.

This reminds me of a hilarious story with my father-in-law, John Martin. When I open my car door, sometimes I need to run after trash that blows out. John never needs to worry about this. His cars are always gleaming and spotless, making this story even funnier. I also needed to wait to print this story until the statute of limitations expired, so nobody would get arrested over it. The story goes as follows:

One day John took a friend away for an errand. To further avoid questions from law enforcement, I won't say which state this happened in. They stopped at a place for only a few minutes, then went back the road they had come in on. In the middle of the road was a freshly hit road killed deer. John's passenger, who we shall leave unnamed, got very excited. He loved venison, and this deer was obviously just recently hit as it hadn't been there 15 minutes before. He begged John to stop and let him load this deer in the back of his van. Loading the deer only took a few minutes, and they were off again. John wasn't too keen on this, as he was worried some deer hair might get on the carpet.

As they continued to their destination John heard a snort, and some thrashing around. Remembering the "dead" deer in the back, this concerned him greatly. He sped up, hoping to quickly get to their destination. They pulled in to their destination, which was actually a counselor's office. Both of them went to the back of the van and opened the doors. The deer was certainly alive and tried to jump out of the van! John's passenger was a big strapping fellow, and he jumped on the deer's back (it was now outside the van). John said he thought the deer was going to run off with the guy on his back! The deer bucked and kicked, while the passenger fellow furiously attempted to finish it off with his dull pocket knife. By now John was expecting the police to show up, but somehow they didn't. The wrestling match lasted a few minutes, with much snorting and shouting. The deer even made some noises too. Finally the deer did expire for real, from exhaustion, car wounds, or the dull pocket knife attack, I'm not sure. It was then thrown into the back of the van, and they quickly continued to John's friend's place, where it was dumped off.

John related it took several hours to clean all the deer blood and hair out of the back of his van. It is not like John to make up stories, and I could hardly believe this account was true! But John assures me it was.

After Mike's gator was hidden in the weeds, we continued on looking for mine. Cliff pointed out a large gator up ahead, and we slowly walked closer, staying behind a raised bank. This gator was indeed big, but a little too big. It would cost over twice as much as a 7-8 footer. I was sorely tempted to just blast the beast, and whip out my credit card. But, being a model of fiscal restraint I passed this up. So Cliff and the rest of us (Marlene, Gina, and Mike were all along too) continued on down the swamp.

The large gator did see us and jumped into the water with a huge splash. I would have had enough time to easily get a shot off though. After hiking awhile, but not really long, Cliff signaled to me he saw a gator in the size range I wanted. We stalked up to a closer dirt bank to check it out.

The gator lay sunning itself in the grass, and Cliff motioned for me to shoot it. Because of the position I was in, I had to hold the gun at an awkward angle. I didn't give this much thought, as it is only a .243 and did not have much recoil. The shot boomed over the swamp, and the alligator hardly twitched. Cliff said, "You got it!", which was good to hear. The gator did roll over with its belly in the air, which must be what they do when they call it quits.

As we walked closer to the bank to attempt to retrieve the gator, Cliff pointed out I had blood running down my face. Sure enough, the scope had popped me right above the eye. Because of the short youth model stock, and the awkward way I was positioned, the recoil shoved the scope into my head. While it sounds good and all to get bloodied up on an alligator hunt,

Above: Lining up to shoot the gator. Right: Watch that scope! Below: Cliff reels in the gator with a treble hook and heavy line.

it's much more macho if the wounds are from gator bites (Cliff has gotten bit twice by gators). The alligator did get the worst end of the deal, as I inadvertently shot off the top of it's head. The plan was to shoot behind the eye, but down far enough to not blow the top of the head off. Cliff assured me if I wanted a head mount the taxidermy company could probably cobble the head back together.

There was a field lane that provided access to the site where we shot the gator, so we waited for Cliff to go get the truck and come back. He did warn us before leaving to keep an eye out for gators on land as "they can sneak up on you." I'm just a little skeptical of that, but hey, I'm all for shooting an extra gator. I wonder if there is a charge if the shooting is in self defense?!

Cliff recounted a hunt with someone looking for a 9 foot gator. They were on foot, in the middle of the swamp in knee deep water (doesn't that sound exciting). The client inadvertently stepped on a submerged gator, which caused it to quickly rise out of the water (probably the client too). The client then shot the gator, which thankfully was the size he was looking for. I thought that hunting trip sounded much more exciting than ours, but I wasn't really sure I was ready to go wade around in alligator infested waters. Initially I thought Cliff must have about the best job in the world, until I thought of the idea of taking complete strangers, who are armed to the teeth, in confrontations with large alligators. I think I'll stick to writing books!

Back at the main office we did a little bit of paperwork (each gator needs to be tagged and recorded) and also took the liberty of posing gators on the limo hood. As soon as we would get the crazy things positioned, their legs would start clawing like crazy, and they would almost fall off the car! My limo hood now has scratches all over it from the gators! Oh well, that just makes for more bragging rights. "Yeah, sorry my car has such an ugly hood, the gators got to it."

One thing about posing with gators: A small gator is really easy to pose with. You just pick it up by the tail, and smile at the camera. A larger gator is a different story. Mine was too heavy for me to just hold up by the tail, and it was also longer than I am tall. All the attempts to pose with my alligator proved very unimpressive, so I had to be happy with the "gator on the limo hood" pose. I did talk Marlene into holding Mike's gator up by the tail for a few photos. No, she did not shoot any gators-yet. Maybe next time we are in Florida! I'm rather proud of her for holding up the dead gator though.

On Saturday we had our book signing at the Pine Craft Park, in Sarasota. This went well, and I met many readers. A couple of people asked me

Above: Cliff tags the gator I shot. Below: Me and my gator. The lighting was terrible, it was a very bright sunny day, causing sharp shadows.

Above: Posing with an 8 foot gator is not easy!
Below: Gators look good on the limo! Right: Marlene is a natural, posing with alligators.

what happened to my head (the cut was very visible), and I explained that I got hit by my scope while shooting an alligator yesterday. That always prompted an interesting response.

Monday morning we headed back down to Outwest Farms for some quality hog hunting. Instead of Marlene and Gina, this time we had Shane, Bryson (Mike's son), and Marlin Eicher along. I was slightly shocked to learn that Marlin's daughter, Rita, had badly wanted to go along. She couldn't because she taught school in Sarasota and apparently the school frowned on teachers taking off short notice to hunt pigs. Shane also had expressed extreme interest in shooting an alligator, so I also added this to our day's itinerary. He didn't mind at all when I told him he had to settle for a smaller gator.

When we arrived at Outwest Farms, we met several other folks who were there to hunt gators. The fellows were from Indiana, I think. Lee was going to take us out on the swamp buggy while Cliff took the other guys out for gators. They were after 12-13 footers! I couldn't wait to see big gators up close, and hoped we would return from hunting at the same time they did.

Shane and Marlin were the first to sit in the "shooters chair." These two chairs were at the front of the buggy. Nobody else was to shoot, just the two guys up front. Lee also had two dogs along to track the hogs. I expected wild pigs to be behind every bush, but it took us about half an hour to find the first one. It bolted out from behind some shrubs, and ran straight away from us. Shane emptied his gun, with big plumes of dust flying up beside the pig, but he missed with every shot. Marlin was using my .50 caliber, and he took a few shots as well. The big muzzle break on the .50 is designed to reduce recoil, which it does well. However, an unwanted side benefit of this is the deafening muzzle blast. During target practice I wear ear plugs and did not even think of this. We all about went deaf on the swamp buggy while Marlin was shooting. Sadly, he didn't hit the pig either.

After that pig ran off and disappeared, Lee let the dogs lose to look for more. In a few minutes the dogs were once again baying and on the chase. We followed in the swamp buggy. If you happen to shoot a dog, it's an automatic $2,000. I made sure Shane knew not to shoot when the dogs were close to any pigs! Lee called the dogs back, and the pig tried to slip away. Shane shot at it, and managed to hit it, putting it down. It was on the small side, smaller than the one he shot in Texas several years ago, but still exciting.

I moved into Shane's seat, since he had his. Marlin wasn't really fond of the 50 caliber, so I switched rifles with him, and he used Shane's .243. We drove around some more in the swamp buggy, and after awhile the dogs

Dust from bullet

Hog Running Away

Above: The hog runs away. The cloud beside it is from a near hit. Below: Marlin shows off the 50 caliber, while Lee drives the swamp buggy.

Above: Shane's pig.

Right: Myself with a red boar. Mary Kate was watching me edit this page, and she said, "I want to shoot a pig too."

That's my girl!

found some more hogs. The first batch of hogs ran out of the brush, but away from us, with the brush in between. We shot at them anyway but didn't hit any of them.

Suddenly one exploded out of the bushes, running in front of us, and Marlin pulled up the .243 and hit it squarely with one shot. The hog flipped head over heels and was down. I told Marlin "that was some fancy shooting!" About this time another hog ran by and hid in a clump of trees. I could just barely make it out, so I threw a few rounds in that direction, hitting it. Climbing off the buggy I got closer on foot, and could see the boar looking at me. It was clacking it's tusks together, and I figured it was probably fairly upset. I'm not really fond of pig meat anyway, so I let the hog have a few more rounds, and this settled it down.

With three hogs down, we had one to go. Mike was up front with his .300 Blackout AR, the same one he used for the gator. After some more driving, we noticed some hogs about 70 yards away. They broke into a dead run, and Mike let loose a volley, taking one down. He pumped a few extra shots into it for good measure. We all had our hogs and ended the hunting that morning. When we arrived back at the main facility, Lee had to run for a bit to go help load the gators the other fellows shot. Indeed, we got a chance to see the big gators up close.

After Lee was finished helping Cliff load up the gators, we headed down to the swamp for Shane's turn at gator hunting. It was still dry, so once again we headed out on foot. There were several small ponds throughout the swamp, and Lee hoped to find a small gator in one of those for Shane. In the event of a non fatal shot, gators are much easier to recover from a small pond. In the main part of the swamp there are many places for them to escape.

It was very windy, and sand was blowing everywhere. Thankfully the sun was out, which helped the gators bask in the sun and be more visible. Soon Lee motioned to a pond up ahead. He had seen some eyes, and could tell by the snout it was around a six foot gator. I was a little worried about Shane's ability to hit the small kill zone behind the eye. He lined up for the gator, lying down on the bank. The blowing wind and sand made it hard for him to concentrate, but he got off a shot. A geyser of water shot up where the gator was, but then the gator disappeared.

We all walked up to the spot where the gator was last seen, and looked around. No gator. Lee started casting his treble hook into the pond, and reeling it across the bottom. After he did this for several minutes Shane and I were starting to despair. But suddenly there was a jerk, and Lee

Pig flipping over

Above: Marlin's crack shot in action. You can see the dust trail the pig was leaving, running wide open. Below: Marlin and his pig, with the rest of us on the swamp buggy.

Above: Mike and his son Bryson pose with their pig. Below: The fearless hunters and our bounty. Actually, I'll admit the skill required is very little, but it is a lot of fun!

shouted that he had it on the line. He told Shane to have his gun ready, as it was still quite alive and would need another shot.

Lee pulled the gator out on the bank, and Shane blasted it at close range, doing quite a bit of damage to the head. We are not sure if Shane hit the gator on the first shot, or just stunned it by hitting the water next to it. But the bottom line is we did get the gator, and Shane was very pleased with it.

After tagging the gator, thanking Lee and his helper (it wasn't Cliff, unfortunately I forget his name) we headed to the taxidermist. Mike's gator was stored there, and we wanted to drop Shane's gator off for some work. Instead of using an ice chest we just put 100 pounds of ice in the limo trunk and threw the gator on top of it. Then we headed back to Sarasota.

A quick plug for Outwest Farms: If you are thinking of going hog hunting or better yet, alligator hunting, give them a call. We have found them to be very professional and easy to work with. Their phone number is 863-634-3262. Their website address is http://www.floridahuntingoutfitter.com. Make sure to tell them we sent you. We don't get a commission, but it makes us feel important.

On Tuesday we had another book signing planned at the park in Pine Craft. I figured that a dead alligator might help draw a crowd, and this proved to be correct. The limo by itself attracts a lot of attention, but when I popped the trunk and showed off the dead gator, people really started coming out of the woodwork. That book signing was our most successful one to date! Note to self: Always keep a dead alligator handy. One guy even nervously asked, "Aren't you afraid the police will show up?!" I guess he thought we might have poached it in the creek beside the park.

That afternoon I met someone I used to work with at Glenwood Foods (over 13 years ago already). His name is Eddie Sensenig. As I was talking to Eddie, a fellow came up and wondered if we were the people doing the blood pressure checks. The other day someone had been there selling vitamins and offering a health check with a little machine you would stick your finger in. Eddie told this guy that all he needed to do was buy our books, and by reading them he would relax and his blood pressure would drop. This particular fellow didn't seem very impressed by this medical advice and left. Eddie's statements have not been confirmed by the FDA! But hey, why not try it? On a more serious note, if you're having trouble with high blood pressure and whatnot, go shoot some alligators. It is very therapeutic.

Above: Shane takes a shot at the gator. The plume of water is right where the gator was, so that is a good sign. Below: Lee gets ready to try and snag the gator. Seeing a heavy duty fishing rod made me feel right at home. I think I have a reel identical to that one in Alaska.

Above: Some large gators! At least 12 footers, maybe 13. Below: At the taxidermy shop, Bryson just so managed to escape the jaws of a gator!

Custom Kitchen Cabinets and Furniture for Your Home

MARC
Mission Aviation Repair Center

Impacting Remote Alaska with the Hope of Jesus Christ through Mission Aviation

Across the vast roadless wilderness of Alaska are hundreds of isolated villages where Americans live in third-world conditions. The rich native culture has been overwhelmed by rampant alcoholism, teen suicide, joblessness, and spiritual darkness. The inhospitable terrain, depressing isolation, high cost of living, inadequate housing, bitter weather, and winter darkness only serve to compound the rapidly changing cultural standards.

Fostering true change is difficult for many villages due to the lack of connecting roads. Exposure and access to Christian influence and care is likewise limited—and sadly, women and children are affected the most.

Less than 100 villages have any established evangelical church, pastor, or missionary presence; and many have no followers of Jesus Christ. When there is a pastor or missionary in the village, they are also isolated and cutoff from the normal spiritual and support networks typically afforded other Christian workers.

Pastors and missionaries in village churches are fighting an uphill battle to share Christ in meaningful ways to an increasingly hard-to-reach population. Missionary Aviation Repair Center has provided a lifeline of hope to these villages, strengthened the ministry of Christians, and expanded the reach of the Gospel across the Alaskan frontier since 1964.

Today, MARC has a fleet of airplanes that fly throughout western Alaska and even across the Bering Sea into eastern Russia. We provide affordable transportation services, training, and quality airplane maintenance for mission organizations through our own internal staff of missionary families who raise their own financial support to serve with MARC. We're privileged to serve God here!

Dwight and Kristin Wenger (and their family) moved to Alaska in the summer of 2016. Dwight works at M.A.R.C. as a mechanic and flight instructor. They are one of the charter families in the church that is starting this summer. Part of the work of this church will probably be outreach to the many remote villages accessible only by air. Dwight works at no charge for M.A.R.C., they live on donations provided by supporters. For more information visit https://www.marcalaska.org/wenger-family.

HOMETOWN OUTDOORS

A PLAIN COMMUNITY PUBLICATIO

Each bimonthly issue of **Hometown Outdoors** packed with exciting stories that range from b game hunting & fishing to a mountain campi trip gone awry.

ALL BACK ISSUES AVAILABLE!

NOVEMBER-DECEMBER 2016

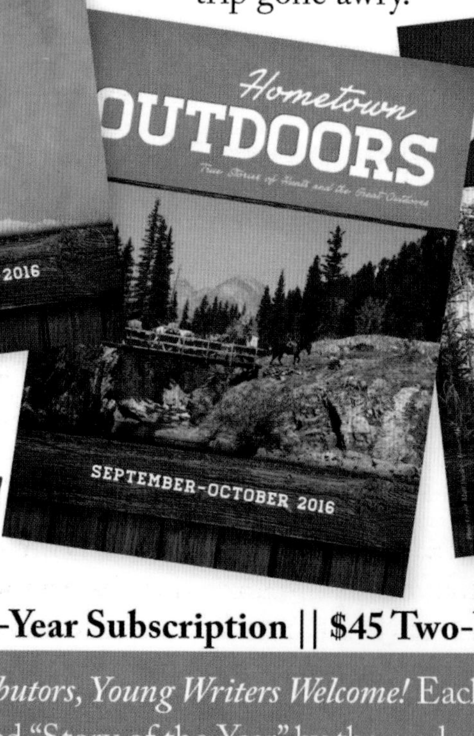

SEPTEMBER-OCTOBER 2016

JANUARY-FEBRUARY 2017

$24 One-Year Subscription || $45 Two-Year Subscription

Needing Contributors, Young Writers Welcome! Each year there is a conte for the best voted "Story of the Year" by the readers with some great pri Get a free One-Year Subscription when you write a story that is featu

To submit an article or subscribe, make check payable and mail to Hometown Outdoors 7578 County Road FF · La Jara, CO 811

You may have noticed I no longer write blog updates on our website. That is because I now write for various publications, and I simply run out of time to write each month. The following two publications I write articles for regularly, so if you enjoyed the blogs, or can't wait for the next book to come out, consider subscribing to these papers. If you own a business you may want to consider placing ads in these publications as well. I advertise our books in both and have been very pleased with the results. A little bit of bragging-the cover photo of the bear in the Jan-Feb 2017 Hometown Outdoors comes from the game camera on my lane in Alaska. You will regularly find Alaska wildlife and pictures from my camera in both publications listed here. And tell them Matt Snader sent you when you call or write them. No, I don't get a commission, but it does make me feel useful.

Plain Communities Business Exchange (PCBE) is a monthly newspaer/magazine featuring stories about manufacturing, farming, and many othr subjects among the plain people. Each month we have theme based stoes, with most of these being written by people with an inside view of the mish Mennonite culture.

We have some great writers that are continually submitting stories on ow to start new businesses, manage cash flow, banking, employee relations nd many more. For your subscription, click on the link below or send a heck to PCBE, PO Box 520, Millersburg PA 17061. Cost is $17.00 for 1 ear (12 copies) mailed to your address.

Other titles by Alaska Adventure Books

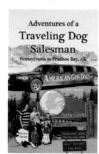

Book 1:
80 Pages, Full Color Photos. 5.5"x8.5"
The Snader's first trip to Alaska in their camouflage limo.
By Matt Snader
$9.99

Book 2:
174 Pages, Full Color Photos. 6"x9"
The Snader's move to Alaska, buying 40 acres site unseen.
By Matt Snader
$12.99

Book 3:
224 Pages, Full Color Photos. 6"x9"
The Snader's first full year as Alaska residents. It is about more than just fishing.
By Matt Snader
$13.99

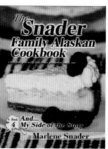

Book 4:
224 Pages, Full color Photos. 7"x9"
Marlene's side of the story, plus over 150 recipes with a photo of each one.
By Marlene Snader
$16.99

Alaska Sea Escapes
124 Pages, B&W 6"x9"
True stories of harrowing escapes at sea in the wild waters of Alaska's fishing industry.
By Wilma Williams
$9.99

Books can be purchased online, or at various retailers around the country.

New for 2017! We have cabins for rent!

Come enjoy 248 acres "off the grid" just down Tall Tree Avenue a mile from my place. Electric is available, provided by solar panels and a generator. We have several RV spots with electric hookup and a dump station. We have two cabins with plumbing, and some smaller cabins with electric only but a shower house is close by. Tent sites are also available. Views of Mt Redoubt and the inlet right from your front porch. About a 25 minute drive from Homer, the "Halibut Capital of the World." For more info call Andy Stoltzfus at 570-989-0078 or visit www.AlaskaLandBarons.com

Note: Quite a few people have asked if I could take them fishing in my boat. I'm very flattered by this, however Alaska law prohibits me accepting <u>any</u> form of payment or reimbursement for fishing services without a guide license. Unfortunately, I can't afford to go fishing every day of the summer. I recommend going fishing with a local charter, I like Ninilchik Saltwater Charters phone # 907-567-3611. Book as far ahead in advance as possible.